How to Create a Successful School

CW01497350

How to Create a Successful School

Francis Beckett

First published in Great Britain in 2010 by
Biteback Publishing Ltd
Heal House
375 Kennington Lane
London
SE11 5QY

ISBN 978-1-84954-016-2

10 9 8 7 6 5 4 3 2 1

A CIP catalogue record for this book is available from the British Library.

Set in Sabon by SoapBox
Printed and bound in Great Britain by
TJ International Ltd, Padstow, Cornwall

Contents

Introduction

This book would not have been written without *The Independent* and the editor of its education pages, Lucy Hodges. In 2007 Lucy commissioned me to write a series of profiles of head teachers. The series has now has been running since September 2007, and most (though not all) of the profiles in this book appeared first in *The Independent*, and benefited from Lucy's thoughtful input. I am very grateful to her for all of this.

In *The Independent*, the early features were confined to 1,500 words and later ones to about 1,100, and I have been glad to take advantage of the greater space allowed by a book to introduce material I would have liked to include in the first place, but could not for lack of space. I have also updated the profiles (except for the six latest ones, which were written in late 2009), and where the head has left, I have taken the opportunity to see how his or her successor is doing.

The reason Lucy and I wanted to have a series of head teacher profiles was that we could see the growing evidence that the crucial element of a successful school is a top class head. Of course you need the best teachers too, but you get nothing else without the right person at the top. An effective head with a clear idea of where he or she is going can bring success out of failure. A head who, however well intentioned, does not have the necessary leadership qualities can snatch failure from the very jaws of success.

That doesn't mean a superhead – a new broom, coming in to sweep out all the rubbish that has gone before, who seems to believe that the history of the school began with his or her arrival. This concept was very popular in the early years of New Labour, when it fitted well with the political atmosphere – Tony Blair was himself a sort of superhead, who apparently believed he was there to sweep out all the rubbish his party had accumulated in a century of muddling along without him.

The trouble with the superhead idea is that, in order for him or her to shine as bright as possible, the school's past has to be painted as black as possible. Many fine retired heads have smarted under the daily denigration they feel they have received from their successors, especially when the nature of the school has been changed – an academy has replaced the school, for example. The superhead is now a widely discredited concept, and several of my interviewees went out of their way to point out that they were not superheads; that though they believed they had improved their schools, their predecessors did some quite good work too.

I looked for successful heads – all of them running ordinary primary or secondary schools to which ordinary families would send their children. I looked for heads who were making a successful job of running difficult schools, and especially for heads who had turned round failing schools. Most of the heads in this book were chosen because they were succeeding against the odds.

Of course there are dozens of others I could have gone to, probably as good and as interesting as case studies as the ones whose doors I arrived at. The process of selection wasn't a scientific one at all, and I would not want anyone to imagine that this book has pretensions to naming Britain's top heads. Some of them I found by the simple process of looking at the winners of such things as Head Teacher of the Year, others by keeping my ear to the ground and finding out who had recently turned a school round, who had dragged his or her school out of a difficult patch, who was being spoken about with respect. I tried not to go to the ones everyone talks of, though, and some famous names do not appear here.

Most books on this sort of subject are written in the dense, impenetrable and slightly disembodied style of education academics, and they repel attempts by the general reader to come to grips with them. This one, by contrast, offers a series of human profiles which demonstrate the feel, the texture of the head teachers and the schools they run: readable portraits of successful heads, describing in layman's language what it is they do and what sort of human beings they are. This book is non-academic and, I hope, accessible. I hope it will help lay members of governing bodies who have to appoint heads. I hope it will appeal to parents trying to negotiate secondary transfer, to help them in judging the local schools on offer. It may also be useful to teachers, heads and prospective heads.

Looking for the non-selective school heads

There were a few self-imposed rules. I did not visit any private fee-charging schools, or any selective schools, or any of the government's new academies. It's not that these do not need good heads – they do – but the skills required are often very different. I wanted to focus on the idea of education as a route out of poverty – education as a great leveller.

In fee-charging schools the problems are very different from those which face the heads in this book. Twenty years ago a distinguished fee-charging school headmaster, Denis Silk, mused publicly on the dilemmas and problems of his calling. 'I remember so clearly the parents of a boy who was in serious trouble saying with clear-eyed naivety: "We simply cannot understand it. He never lacked for anything. We gave him everything he asked for and still he wasn't satisfied."' Silk spoke about the 'straight and simple' questions he asked himself to ensure he was doing his job properly. One of them was: 'Have I funked telling a parent that he has given his son too much money and too little of his time?' An important question, no doubt, for those who spend their lives educating the children of the rich, but a dilemma which the teachers in whom I am interested are seldom likely to face.

(Incidentally, I use the description 'fee-charging schools' not out of political prejudice, but for the sake of accuracy. These schools are commonly, and inaccurately, called independent schools. Most of them these days are not independent at all; they belong to chains of schools, some of which are very centralised, controlling their heads far more than central or local government controls the heads of state schools. In addition, fee-charging schools are in no sense more independent than academies – like academies, they have limited independence from the dictates of local and central government, and they are not publicly owned. The difference between them and academies is that they charge fees and academies do not. The other common description – 'fee-paying schools' – is even more inaccurate than 'independent schools'. They do not pay fees; they charge them.)

Fee-charging schools are for the well off. So, in a different way, are selective schools, which is why none of Britain's 165 remaining grammar schools finds a place here. Grammar schools, as the pressure group Comprehensive Future says, 'admit few pupils from low-income families. Statistics show that their intake is skewed towards the better off, some of whom receive expensive private coaching to help them pass the eleven-plus.'

This coaching really does exclude the poor, partly because they cannot afford it, and partly because they may not know it is there. One of many successful companies offering coaching boasts

> flexible eleven-plus tuition in maths, English, verbal and non-verbal reasoning. Home visits, one-to-one and small group tutorials (maximum five pupils) means Tuition for You work around you to ensure your child is sufficiently prepared for their selective exams. Pupils are taught in Tuition for You's friendly, homely environment with a close-knit structure of experienced and qualified tutors, or if you prefer, a tutor can travel to you, and your child can be taught in the comfort of their own home, using a varied selection of materials and resources.

Unsurprisingly, given all this, grammar schools have a far lower proportion of children who are poor enough to qualify for free school meals than the nearby schools which are required to take the children the grammar schools do not want to teach. It is true that a small number of children from low-income families trace their route out of poverty to passing the eleven-plus and going to a grammar school. But a great many more have their route effectively blocked by failing the exam and being consigned to the schools for failures, which, no matter what they are called, are effectively secondary moderns.

As evidence of this, I cite Professor Richard Pring of Oxford University's Department of Educational Studies. He passed the eleven-plus and went to the local grammar school, which convinced him of the need to get rid of them. 'One thing I have remained passionate about is the injustice of early selection,' he said in 2000, in an interview for a book called *The School of Tomorrow*, by Roger Crombie White. I cite also Dr William Poole, who wrote to the *Daily Telegraph* on 18 May 2007:

> As an eleven-plus failure, who eventually gained a PhD including, along the way, an offer of a postgraduate place at Oxford, I noticed one rather glaring mistake in the popular argument about the role of grammar schools in enhancing 'educational opportunity'. Whilst grammar schools have traditionally provided a very good standard of education – and of that there can be little doubt – the real problem is that this applies only for a minority of any generation. The elephant in the room consists of the genuinely appalling standard of education provided for the great majority of kids in the secondary modern schools – which are and were a national disgrace.

But Dr Poole might accept that this is not the fault of the secondary modern schools themselves, and for this book I have gone to the heads of two secondary moderns in areas which still run the eleven-plus examination. Derek Davies in Trafford, Manchester, and William Cotterell in Kent both run schools which take the children the local grammar schools do not wish to teach, and I asked them how they start to overcome the idea of failure

which is embedded in their pupils from day one. Their answers
are, I think, among the most interesting things here.

Academies are a greyer area. I am personally opposed to them
– I once wrote a book called *The Great City Academy Fraud* – and
they are allowed to select 10 per cent of their intake. But many of
them do not select, and are proper comprehensive schools, helping
to make education a route out of poverty. However, the trouble
is that other schools cannot easily follow the example of the
academies, because their state funding is much less generous. In
2005 the Parliamentary Select Committee on Education reported:

> The capital cost of academies is significantly beyond that
> of other new schools. The academies currently in operation
> generally provide places for around 1,200 students in each
> school. At an average cost of £25 million per school, this
> represents a cost of almost £21,000 per place. In contrast,
> the government's basic need cost multipliers for building new
> secondary school accommodation is [*sic*] just under £14,000
> per place. It is equally important to note that although
> academies are planned to take large numbers of pupils
> eventually, they often begin with small rolls and some build
> up from a Year 7-only intake in their first year of operation.
> This increases the cost per pupil far beyond the cost per
> place.

At first academies were said to be going to cost £10 million
each, which made the sponsor's £2 million sound like a respectable
contribution. But because sponsors were allowed to choose
everything, and virtually given an open cheque against the public
purse, the average cost for each of the first twelve academies was
£23 million, and later ones have cost a lot more than that (though
costs are now being belatedly reined in.) The Bexley Business
Academy, the most expensive of the lot, had a capital budget
of £35.9 million, and has easily over-spent on it. The sponsor's
contribution has remained capped at £2 million. Even though
recent academies have cost less – Bexley was a shock to the system

– academies are eating up far more than their fair share of the education budget, which harms neighbouring schools and tends to counteract any good they may be doing.

And academies, like fee-charging schools, are generally parts of a chain of schools which controls their heads fairly rigorously. Some of these chains, such as the United Learning Trust (ULT), are highly centralised, so that the school heads have only a little more autonomy than the manager of your local branch of Tesco. One ULT head once told me he could not speak to me without 'permission from Head Office'. Once, after I had interviewed John Murphy, the head teacher of one of the academies run by the Christian academy sponsor Oasis, Steve Chalke, who founded and controls Oasis, introduced me to his director of education with the words 'This is John Murphy's line manager'. The heads in this book all report to governing bodies, of course, and all have some relationship with their local authority, but none of them have anyone they could properly refer to as their line manager. They run their schools. Within the demands of central government and the national curriculum, they control what goes on there.

So in this book I am focusing on primary and secondary schools with a (more or less) non-selective intake, mostly in areas with high unemployment or high levels of poverty. The reason is that these schools perform perhaps the hardest and certainly the most vital task of any school – for without them, many of their pupils would get no education at all. They represent the only chance in life these pupils are likely to be offered.

Education – a route out of poverty or a poverty trap?

I wanted to focus on education as a route out of poverty, which, at its best, is what it is. Providing a route out of poverty is the first and greatest benefit of education. A child in a household living below the poverty line is less likely than other children to succeed at school, and to gain the qualifications which allow him or her to escape from poverty. The children of the poor are less likely to get places at selective schools, less likely to do well in public examinations and gain qualifications, and less likely to attend university.

Far too often, though, what schools actually do is perpetuate a cycle of low income and low expectations. All studies persistently find that the gap is getting wider. One recent such study comes from the Sutton Trust. Its 2009 report *Attainment Gaps between Pupils in the Most Deprived and Advantaged Schools* found:

› Pupils eligible for free school meals (FSM) at some point in their schooling in the most deprived 10 per cent of schools on average achieve two grades less in their best eight GCSEs than FSM pupils in the most advantaged 10 per cent of schools, after individual factors (ethnicity, social background, prior attainment) are taken into account.

› Pupils not eligible for FSM in the most deprived 10 per cent of schools on average achieve 2½ grades less in their best eight GCSEs than non-FSM pupils in the most advantaged 10 per cent of schools, after individual factors are taken into account.

› Pupils are more likely to enter vocational examinations in the most deprived schools than those in more advantaged schools. For example, they are five to six times more likely to enter a GNVQ.

› Highly academically able pupils (the 10 per cent highest attainers at age eleven) in the most deprived 10 per cent of schools on average achieve half a grade less per GCSE examination than high-ability pupils in the most advantaged 10 per cent of schools, after individual factors are taken into account.

› Highly able pupils attending the most deprived schools were ten times more likely to take an intermediate GNVQ than high-ability pupils in the most advantaged schools.

› High-attaining pupils attending the most deprived schools face a double penalty – they enter fewer full GCSE examinations (not vocational equivalents or half GCSEs) and achieve about half a grade less per full GCSE examination entered.

› In 2006, 13.6 per cent of secondary school pupils in England were eligible for FSM in their GCSE year. However, an additional 7.7 per cent – the 'hidden poor' – were eligible for FSM at some point during their secondary school career.

› The GCSE attainment of the 'hidden poor' was found to be slightly lower than the attainment of those who were eligible for FSM in their GCSE year.

› 22 per cent of 'ever FSM' pupils attain five A*–C GCSEs including English and maths compared with 52 per cent of 'never FSM' pupils – an attainment gap of 30 percentage points. This is larger than the equivalent 28-point gap between FSM and non-FSM pupils, the government's preferred measure.

Moving on from GCSE results, of 135,000 students with As and A*s at A-level in 2007, just 189 were poor enough to qualify for FSM.

In November 2009 the University and College Union released a study of educational achievement by parliamentary constituency, showing that people from traditionally under-achieving areas are proportionately less likely to have a degree in 2009 than they were in 2005. This report, *Location, Location, Location: The Widening Education Gap in Britain and How Where You Live Determines Your Chances*, shows that two out of three people in middle-class Sheffield Hallam have a degree, and only 3 per cent have no qualifications at all. But just down the road in poor and working-class Sheffield Brightside, almost a quarter have no qualifications and just 15 per cent have a degree. In the twenty constituencies with the highest level of participation in higher education, the average proportion of the working-age population with a degree-level qualification increased from 48.8 per cent in 2005 to 57.2 per cent in 2008.

Conversely, poor constituencies have seen academic achievement decline. Between 2005 and 2008, in the twenty constituencies with the lowest level of participation in higher education, the average proportion of the working-age population with a degree-level qualification and above fell from 12.6 per cent to 12.1 per cent.

And poor qualifications result in unemployment or low-paid work: as the Joseph Rowntree Foundation has noted, 'the "employment gap" for those with the lowest level of qualifications compared to the average remains one of only three government indicators on social exclusion going in the wrong direction'. A 2009 Joseph Rowntree study finds that 'children growing up in poverty and disadvantage are less likely to do well at school. This feeds into disadvantage in later life and in turn affects their children.'

Unsurprisingly, therefore, fee-charging school pupils are more likely to be successful in later life. Britain still has a kind of hereditary ruling elite. In 2009 the Sutton Trust investigated the scholastic backgrounds of more than 1,700 fellows of the Royal Society and the British Academy and found that nearly half of them came from the one in fourteen of the population who attended fee-charging schools. One in four university vice-chancellors attended fee-charging schools, as did a third of MPs, half our doctors and nearly three quarters of our judges. The more prestigious the university, the smaller its proportion of students from poor families.

The 7 per cent who attend fee-charging schools still account for about half the intake of Oxford and Cambridge universities. And these universities supply those who run the country. Gordon Brown is the first Prime Minister to have attended a university other than Oxford or Cambridge since Sir Henry Campbell-Bannerman, who died in office in 1908, almost 100 years before Brown became Prime Minister. (A few, such as Churchill, Callaghan and Major, did not go to university at all.)

To see the result of generations of under-achievement, look at any prison. A 2007 report from the Prince's Trust, *The Cost of Exclusion: Counting the Cost of Youth Disadvantage in the UK*, by Sandra McNally and Shqiponja Telhaj says:

Prisoners have very low levels of basic skills compared with the rest of the population. The position is even worse for

prisoners between eighteen and twenty years of age whose
basic skills, unemployment and social exclusion background
are all over a third worse than that of older prisoners . . .
under-achievement at school appears to increase the
probability of turning to crime and negatively affects the
health and emotional well-being of the individuals concerned.
With youth crime costing upwards of £1 billion and public
costs for treating depression at between £11 and £28 million,
the total bill for educational under-achievement is undeniably
huge.

The education system should be what stands between poor
children and their dismal legacy. So governments and educational
institutions produce a stream of ideas designed to help the poor
benefit from education: examples are Sure Start, schemes for top
universities to attract applications from inner city comprehensives,
and recent proposals to target specific ethnic communities
in schools.

Yet the problem remains, obstinate and intractable. So is it
structural? Is our state education system designed to perform this
vital task in the war against poverty? Or are our schools – and in
particular our secondary schools – part of the problem, not part
of the solution?

As a journalist, I have always looked at this question from
the top down, studying political arguments, statistics and
international comparisons, and talking to eminent educationalists
and politicians. This has not produced much by way of solutions,
and it is time to look at it from the bottom up, by writing in
detail about real people, schools, heads, teachers, families and
neighbourhoods.

I am starting with heads. There is of course a great deal more
to look at. In one sense, this book can only scratch the surface.
To understand, really understand, what is going on, we need the
colour and texture not just of the schools and their heads and
teachers, but also of the neighbourhoods and communities they
serve, the lives lived by the pupils, their families, their teachers

and their communities. We need something like *The Bitter Cry of Outcast London*, written by the Rev. Andrew Mearns in 1883. Before Mearns studied the way the poor lived, the Victorian middle class already had the statistics of poverty. What Mearns added was the texture of poverty, as it was endured by human beings in teeming slums.

We need something of the power of Mearns's descriptions for our own time and our own inner cities:

> Tens of thousands are crowded together . . . To get into [the slums] you have to penetrate courts reeking with poisonous and malodorous gases arising from accumulations of sewage and refuse scattered in all directions and often flowing beneath your feet . . . Up rotten staircases . . . Down dark and filthy passages swarming with vermin . . . [to] the dens in which [live] these thousands of beings who belong, as much as you, to the race for which Christ died . . . In one cellar [live] a man ill with smallpox, his wife just recovering from her eighth confinement, and the children running about half naked and covered with dirt. Here are seven people living in one underground kitchen, and a little dead child lying in the same room. Elsewhere is a poor widow, her three children, and a child who had been dead thirteen days. Her husband, who was a cabman, had shortly before committed suicide.

An updated version of Mearns will look at how children learn in the poorest parts of our inner cities, the barriers against them escaping and the pressures which ensure that the cycle of poverty will continue down the generations. This book looks at one aspect only.

One writer has made a start on the sort of work that is needed, by providing a detailed portrait of one inner city school, its teachers, its children, its parents and its community. The education journalist Wendy Wallace spent six months at Edith Neville School, with an overwhelmingly Muslim intake, in a deprived area of London known as Somers Town, between St Pancras and Euston stations, 'a dense and parochial urban village with old council houses all around it'. The result was her 2005 book *Oranges and Lemons: Life in an Inner City Primary School*. She defied the conventions governing education books: that they should be stuffed with phrases like 'learning outcomes' and be written to support one or other of the competing ideologies: for example, to prove that privatisation is either a good thing or a bad thing; or to add some new special pleading to the phonics versus real books debate.

Like all the best writers, Wallace builds a picture from small details, sticking to the storyteller's principle: show, don't tell. Here is a little girl: 'Maharun's brown prosthetic eyes are so realistic that when she focuses her attention on someone she appears to be looking right at them. But her blindness is total; born without eyes, she has no real concept of seeing.' She does not tell us in general terms that such schools are kept pitifully short of money. Instead she writes:

> This year the amount they have to spend is down in real terms by about £100,000. 'Please pay Joan for your personal phone calls,' reads a notice on her wall. But the minor economies in place all over the school – staff paying for their own tea, coffee and personal photocopying, buying materials for projects out of their own pocket – are not enough. They have balanced the books this year by not replacing a departing teacher whose job was supporting children with English as a second language.

She does not tell us that the policy of handing school meal provision to the lowest bidder results in children getting an unappetising and unhealthy diet. Instead she provides a description of the food, and the way it is served, which made me feel ill; and she tells us how much money the school is permitted to spend on what is, for many of these children, the main meal of the day.

From this book, you get one of the most sympathetic and

minutely drawn portraits of a school head, with all his troubles and pressures, that I have read anywhere. Head teacher Sean O'Regan was born in 1964 in rural Cork, but his parents soon moved to Jersey, where he attended the primary school of which his mother was head teacher. He took an Oxford degree and a Reading teaching qualification, and went to Edith Neville as a 26-year-old class teacher in 1990. Seven years later, he was the head, when it was at the bottom of the borough's league tables. Today it does well in league tables and Ofsted calls it 'a highly effective school with a number of excellent features'. Mr O'Regan is still there. 'I'm not *a* head teacher,' he says. 'I'm *the* head teacher of Edith Neville School.' His wife is a Muslim whom he started dating when she came to teach at the school.

In what had been a very traditionally run school, he wanted to bring in a child-friendly culture and raise standards at the same time. Wallace testifies to the fact that he achieved both. But she also shows us the day-to-day grind. Here is her description of the head's morning conference:

> Later in the day the head will be attending a child protection conference, he tells his staff. A couple are applying to have their daughter removed from the at-risk register. 'She's still covered in bruises,' interrupts a teacher, clearly upset. 'She's still dirty. Still hungry.' Her mobile phone goes off inside her bag and she reaches down into it with both hands, flustered.

I have returned to O'Regan in this book, to see how the years since 2005 have treated him.

Extending Wallace's method to the whole country is the next task – a book which will help us towards answers to such questions as these: What is the effect on poverty of different types of school – grammar schools, comprehensive schools, foundation schools, fee-charging schools, the new academies? What is the effect on low-income families of government attempts to promote parental choice? What conclusions do we draw from the fact that most 'failing' schools, as defined by Ofsted, are in troubled inner city areas? What conclusions do we draw from the fact that faith schools tend not to be failing, even when many of their pupils are poor? Does this argue for more faith schools or fewer? Does it mean that faith schools are managing to avoid failure, or that they are finding a way of forcing other schools to educate the more difficult children?

But answering these is just a step on the way to the big questions: What is the effect of a history of low achievement in a family and a community, and how can this be counteracted? Does the education system fail people from low-income households and disadvantaged groups, and what can be done to change this? How is education perceived by different people on low incomes? What is the effect of factors like ethnic origin, the values of the local community, parents' experience of education, the educational history of the area?

And these in turn lead to the biggest question of all: What is the relationship between poverty and educational failure?

The answers may not always be what I expect. As a journalist writing about education, I look at statistics which show, for example, that grammar schools have only a tiny proportion of children eligible for free school meals compared with comprehensive schools; and at the 2002 OECD international survey shows that comprehensives can produce social cohesion and good results. From these I draw the conclusion that the supporters of grammar schools are wrong to say they provide a route out of poverty; rather, Britain's remaining 165 grammar schools embed poverty where it is. But is that right? Or does it have all the faults of a conclusion reached from the journalist's top-down way of looking at things?

Again, as a journalist I look at the high exclusion rates from city academies, at the background of the excluded children (disproportionately from deprived homes), and draw the conclusion that these new schools, in using their powers of exclusion, are helping to perpetuate a cycle of poverty. Other journalists, equally simplistically, draw the conclusion that they are protecting other children's power to learn, and that therefore these exclusions are helping many children to escape poverty. Am I right, or are my colleagues right? Or are we both half right? Until we understand the lives of the excluded low-income children, we will not know for certain.

Donald Hirsch has argued powerfully that the failure to reform the examination system along the lines of the Tomlinson report – the 2004 report which proposed revolutionary changes in education between the ages of fourteen and nineteen – was a missed opportunity 'to abolish the sharp divide between those who succeed and fail at sixteen: the "sheep and goats" of our education system'. The failures are, disproportionately, the poor students. But how do they see the examination system – as an obstacle or an incentive?

Whatever the answers, there's a simple, stark truth about our society. Poverty is inherited. People get it from their parents. The best head teachers for the schools in the poorest areas are a necessary, but not a sufficient, requirement to put this right. So studying how they work, what they do and what they think is a necessary, but not a sufficient, requirement for a better society which does not embed failure and poverty in families and communities.

What can we learn from these head teachers?

The schools whose heads I profiled are those which, more than anything else yet invented, stand between the poor and this dismal legacy of poverty. I looked for heads who were making a successful job of running difficult schools and educating children in whose families disadvantage and poverty had become embedded, and for heads who had turned round failing schools. Each of the heads profiled in this book was chosen partly because he or she was succeeding against the odds – whether the odds were a special measures verdict from Ofsted or (in one case) leading a school through the trauma of having the building burn down.

I hope these profiles will help teachers, heads and school governors to find out what are the skills, attributes, habits of thought, qualities and attitudes required. I hope that these profiles help towards an understanding of what successful school leadership is. But I also hope that they are easy reading for the lay reader with no specialist professional knowledge of education, as portraits of exceptional human beings doing startling things in interesting and innovative schools. I have therefore avoided education jargon wherever possible, except occasionally to mock it.

So does this book tell you what qualities, attributes and methods make a successful head teacher? No, it doesn't, because there isn't a formula. The heads in this book are very different, and their recipes for success are also very different. But some common themes emerged.

One is rebellion. Many of the heads in this book – though not all by any means – are rebels, with a healthy contempt for all the things they are supposed to revere.

There is the activist, campaigning Phil Cross at Hurlingham and Chelsea School: 'In his first year as head at Hurlingham and Chelsea, Phil Cross got it out of special measures. In his second year, he set it on a path of steeply rising exam results. In his third, he fought off a proposal to close the school.' Cross does not mind in the slightest if his views run directly counter to educational orthodoxy. He says of his pupils: 'You get them all, in their uniforms, in the classroom, the teacher starts work, and thirty hands go up. "Sir, I haven't got a pen." So we provided biros. Why have an argument over a pen that costs 10 pence? Now we will move to saying "Bring them in".'

There is Sue Seifert, who started rebelling in the 1960s when she trained as a teacher at the Froebel Institute, argued about everything, and got a reference from the institute saying she was unfit to be a teacher. Fortunately, it arrived late, and the Inner London Education Authority had already given her a job. Her style of leadership is so far away from current orthodoxy that I can't understand how Seifert gets away with it. Neither can she.

There is the American Paul Kelley of Monkseaton Community High School on Tyneside, who, while Sue Seifert was being told she was unfit to teach, was being arrested for demonstrating against the Vietnam War, and who will probably always be remembered as the Laura Spence head. At the end of the 1990s, Laura, one of his sixth-formers, was accepted by top universities all over the world and was offered a scholarship at Harvard – but she was turned down by Oxford University. A tutor's note said she might not fit in because she lacked confidence 'as with other comprehensive school pupils'. Kelley says she did not lack confidence, and the Laura Spence affair became a *cause célèbre* when he complained; his complaint reached the ears of the then Chancellor Gordon Brown, who called the Oxford decision a disgrace.

But there is much more to Kelley than Laura Spence. For a start, there is a head with no office, just a desk in a vast central open-plan area where anyone can wander up and talk to him. Behind him as he sits at his desk is the staff room, which has windows so that everyone can see what is going on inside. In most schools, teachers would worry about pupils seeing them relaxing, but pupils at Monkseaton High School have learned that the sight of a teacher drinking tea is terminally boring.

Before Kelley arrived, no pupil at Monkseaton had gone to any of Britain's top universities; now there's a steady trickle. Laura Spence was his second Harvard scholarship: Laura Dixon won one the previous year. It helps, of course, that their American head knew the US system, but as he says, 'every head brings what he's got to the job'.

Kelley thinks Ofsted and the government are a ball and chain for the ambitious head: Ofsted judges schools 'in an antiquated, expensive and inaccurate way' while politicians 'focus on education and stamp their prejudices (or those of the swing voters) onto it'. Unrepentant at causing the government embarrassment over Laura Spence, he has found several more ways of making the British establishment foam at the mouth. He has irritated the Church of England with his demand to be allowed to run a secular school, free from the ministrations of the Standing Advisory Council on Religious Education, which tells schools how to teach religion. 'A child has the right to be introduced to all views, including the secular one,' he says. 'It is not the function of schools to promote a particular religious or political belief.' He mentions, deadpan, that the choice is either making education formally secular, as in France and the USA, or formally religious, as in Britain and Iran. He's been told he must run a Christian assembly, but he refuses to do so, for which defiance Ofsted routinely deducts points from the school's score. He can afford that because his results are so good. For if a head chooses to be a rebel, he or she has to make sure that the school's results are so good that they can get away with it. The lesson is that, so long as your results are very good indeed, you can afford to stick two fingers up at the establishment.

This lesson has been absorbed especially strongly by David Nichols in Derby. Because Nichols, tall and dark suited, looks and sounds a little like a provincial bank manager, it takes the visitor a moment or two to realise that the things he says are often incendiary. 'We only became a specialist school because the government gives you money to do that. I don't like the idea, I think it's fundamentally wrong. Comprehensive schools should excel in all subjects. We're proud of all our subject teaching here.' There goes one government sacred cow. Another was casually murdered when a form arrived on his desk from the Department for Children, Schools and Families offering a dollop of government money if he could show how he was going to 'transform' his school. Ever since Sir Cyril Taylor launched the academy programme, 'transforming' schools has been New Labour dogma – you can never change a school, you have to transform it – but Nichols rightly thinks he runs a fine school which does not require 'transforming'. He wanted the funding, but still said on the form that his school did not need to be 'transformed'. He got the money anyway. In 2009 he helped scupper the government's determination to have two of its prized academies in Derby – so a third sacred cow hits the abattoir. You can read how he did it in the profile in this book.

Nichols had better keep his exam results up, or swift and terrible retribution will be visited upon him.

Less wholehearted rebels are the London heads Jo Shuter and Jo Dibb. They do not come straight out with it, as Derek Nichols would do, and they wrap it up in careful diplomatic language. This is probably the result of being in the political cauldron of London education. Shuter was, after all, Tony Blair's favourite head, though this should not necessarily be held against her, and she has had to deal with the over-sensitive and fiercely sectarian public relations department at Westminster City Council, which had a tendency to pounce on any statement that looked like criticism of its policies, however mild. Dibb's criticism of the policy of building a better-resourced academy next door to her school has all the caution of a London head, walking the capital's political tightrope in the sure knowledge that there are unexploded bombs everywhere: 'Whenever you have schools differentially resourced you have dislocation.' I think she meant: 'Give one school a lot more government money than its neighbour and you're asking for trouble.' But she is too skilled an operator to put it that crudely.

Rebellion is fuelled by the feeling of many heads that government ministers pontificate about schools without ever bothering to listen to the people who run them and who know how they work. This is, of course, a trait among senior politicians, who tend to suppose that there are two sorts of skill: the sort they possess, and the sort that isn't worth bothering with. In 2001 the Department for Education asked all local authorities and a sample of 1,000 primary schools whether it was reasonable to set a target of 85 per cent of children reaching level 4 in Key Stage 2 tests in English and maths. No, said the schools, it was not reasonable, but the target was set anyway, and, naturally, not met.

Rebellion is also fuelled by the idea that governments can somehow 'transform' schools by tinkering with the way in which they are governed and funded – an illusion often shared by local education authorities, academy sponsors and other education bureaucrats, but seldom by the people who actually do the educating. A 2007 press release from the governors at Fortismere School in north London began: 'The Fortismere Governing Body is proceeding with its plans to raise standards at the school by

changing the category of the school to foundation, following
a widespread month-long public consultation which solicited
responses from families, staff, other local schools, trade unions,
MPs, the local authority and other stakeholders.'

Changing the nature and governance of the school,
the favoured solution among politicians, seldom helps and
frequently does harm. It's heads and teachers that make the
difference. Schools adjudicator Sir Philip Hunter, in a 2008
interview with Peter Wilby for *The Guardian*, said: 'It's very easy
to invent a new kind of school. You come up with a name, play
around with the governing body, decide who owns the land and
appoints the staff, and decide how funding gets to it. That's it.'
And so it is. Easy, and entirely pointless. Hunter, with two other
chief education officers, invented foundation schools in twenty
minutes in the Tate Gallery tea room.

Good primary school heads seem, on my partial and
unscientific sample, to be less inclined to rebellion than their
secondary school counterparts. In St Ives, Cornwall, Sue Smith's
style is careful, thoughtful and above all well researched, but not
at all rebellious. Philip Friend's first advice to a head is to take the
Ofsted visit very, very seriously, and he actually thinks the process
of preparing for it helps a head to identify things that he or she
ought to be doing anyway.

One thing all the heads in this book share is a passion to ensure
that the best education should not be confined to and corralled by
the rich. All of them, to some extent, are responsible for educating
the poor, and all of them share Paul Kelley's conviction that there
is nothing the most expensive fee-charging school offers which
they cannot offer in their schools, except snob value. It's an article
of faith, an absolute determination. It's what drives them.

In Harrow, Janice Howkins points out that there are a few big,
expensive houses near her school, Bentley Wood, but the children
from those homes mostly go to fee-charging schools (one of them
being the famous establishment nearby which educated Winston
Churchill) – and, she says, their parents are wasting their money:
there is nothing an expensive school can give them that Bentley

Wood can't offer. Jo Dibb says that down the road from her school, Elizabeth Garrett Anderson School in north London, is a prestigious, expensive and selective fee-charging girls' school. 'I say to parents that if you went there you would be paying £12,400 a year, and extra for this, extra for that. But you can't get a better education anywhere than you get here.'

Yet, Dibb adds, in spite of all this, the fee-charging schoolgirls do have an advantage. 'There are girls who leave EGA with a string of A*s, but if a girl from a private school and a girl from EGA walked into this room now, both equally bright, with equal qualifications, you would know straight away which was which.' The reason is 'the confidence of class'. Upper-middle-class girls know how to appeal to upper-middle-class Oxbridge admissions tutors, which is why Oxbridge still takes about half its intake from the 7 per cent of the population which goes to fee-charging schools.

All these head teachers are determined to make their state schools as good as fee-charging schools, but there is no sort of unanimity among them about how it is to be done. Jo Shuter at Quintin Kynaston School in north London thinks uniforms for pupils, and suits for staff, matter terribly, but just a few miles round the North Circular Road, primary school head Sue Seifert of Montem School thinks the opposite, and practises what she preaches. When I saw her, she was wearing what she always wore, and it could not have been less like power dressing if she had avoided it deliberately. But I do not think she was avoiding it; it simply would not have occurred to her to dress in what most people now think is the part. She did not subscribe to the currently modish view that you cannot learn unless you are dressed to learn. It's hard to see how Seifert could be less fashionable. And the same applied to the language she used. She simply does not do phrases like 'drive standards up' or 'restructure my management team' or even 'deliver quality education'.

Somewhere down the middle comes Phil Cross, who thinks uniforms matter most when you are turning round a failing school. 'All the time the battle is about the uniform, it's not about something else,' he told me. 'It's the front line.'

But some common themes emerged, as the heads profiled provided some of the lessons to be learned in their own words. Cross said: 'I want teachers who love working with children. We can sort out the rest. But if you don't like children this job must be horrible.' I think all the heads in this book agree with that. They are all light years away from the sort of distant authority figure that was common in schools when I grew up in the late 1950s and early 1960s, and is still to be found in a few educational backwaters – these days, oddly, most frequently in selective grammar schools: the dark-suited chalky pedagogues of my childhood.

It's a short step from liking children to the conviction that you have to treat them with respect. Kevin Harcombe of Redlands Primary School in Hampshire said to me: 'Sometimes a child comes from another school with a dreadful reputation for behaviour, but he's a pussycat here because we treat him with respect and expect respect back.'

Harcombe identified another common theme which emerged from all of the interviews: 'high expectations is the key'. This was put to me in its starkest form by Derek Davies, who is especially interesting, for Stretford High School in Trafford, near Manchester, is a secondary modern school: they still have eleven-plus examinations in Trafford, so his pupils arrive knowing that the education system has already branded them as failures. Davies tells his pupils: 'Whatever you want, you can achieve it, if you want it that badly.' He says the same thing in different ways from the day they arrive as eleven-plus failures until they leave at sixteen (for Stretford High School has no sixth form). 'When they come here I talk to them straight away, even in Year 7, about going to university' he says. 'Self-esteem, self-belief – we work very hard on this.'

Another common, but not universal, theme is showmanship. Derek Davies, the theatre director manqué, is the most overt showman in this collection; to watch his slight, trim figure, shoulders thrown back, topped with an almost pixie-like face, smiling broadly, marching round the corridors of his school, saying

'Good morning' to everyone he meets and insisting on the courtesy of a reply, is to see someone impose enthusiasm and drive and ambition by sheer force of will and personality.

Though Davies is the most obvious performer in this collection, he is very far from being the only one. Jo Shuter is another. There's a real cult of personality at Quintin Kynaston School. You hear the occasional complaint about it, but it works. Shuter admits it cheerfully. She is probably the closest thing we have in this book to a 'hero head' – she places herself at the centre of the changes she wishes to see. It works for her and her school.

But showmanship is just one style of doing things, and it doesn't suit everyone. It works if that's how you are built – it comes naturally to Davies and Shuter – but the opposite can work just as well, as Janice Howkins in Harrow proved to me. I told her that most of the successful heads I had interviewed were natural performers whose noisy extrovert characters are an integral part of their professional personas, but that she appeared quiet, thoughtful, even a little shy. But she, too, insists that she acts, and I saw what she meant. She walks the corridors exuding a sort of friendly, quiet authority which the girls respond to; she does not make a special effort to draw attention to herself, as Davies or Shuter would do, but she does not need to. She quoted the former London schools commissioner Tim Brighouse approvingly: the head, he said, is like the conductor of an orchestra – if she can walk away and it goes on playing, she is doing a good job.

One other thing seemed to unite many, though not all, of these successful heads: an unhappy experience of their own education. It is easy to see how that might make a person want to go into teaching and see if things could be done better. As it happens, I did just that as a young man. I had spent four years under the thumb of the Jesuits, having snobbery and religious bigotry beaten into me. The head was a distant authority figure, even though the school had only just over 200 boys in it. He always seemed to me to be a fairly benign sort of priestly cove, but he was not in any way in touch with what went on in the corridors of the school he ran. Of course he was the least of the problems – it was a school where the teaching was lazy and didactic, and bullying was not so much tolerated as encouraged by a system which allowed older boys formally to beat younger ones.

Years later, when I graduated, I felt an urge to go into the state system and find out what real educators did. I taught for a year, at a comprehensive school in south London and a secondary modern in Newcastle-under-Lyme. The care and thought that many of the teachers I met put into their work was a revelation to me. I learned that I did not have the talent to bring out the best in the children who attend these schools, or even to teach them effectively. But I also learned how to recognise that talent when I saw it.

Something similar happened to a surprisingly large number of the heads in this book. Philip Friend set out consciously to create the opposite of the primary school he attended in a south Wales mining village, from which he remembers only playing football and being bullied. He was unhappy there, and failed the eleven-plus. He keeps a mug in his office bearing a picture of that school – a Victorian brick building blackened by coal dust – to remind himself of what the primary school he heads, Eccleston Mere, must never become. Jo Shuter, a clever girl from a comfortably off north London Jewish family, was destined either for a selective grammar school or a very splendid fee-charging school until she deliberately failed her eleven-plus so that she could go to the local comprehensive, and she rebelled there instead.

The other thing a head must have is a degree of political skill. The head is the person who stands between their staff and children on the one hand, and the politicians and bureaucrats on the other. Only the head can create a safe refuge where he or she can get on with the job without suddenly finding themselves in the eye of a political storm. 'I'm not a politician at all,' Jo Dibb said to me with a self-deprecating laugh, and I knew I was in the presence of one of the most sophisticated political operators in London education.

And if you want proof, look at the profiles in this book of Des Smith and Paul Patrick, who were both hugely successful heads. There's no argument about that, you just have to look at their results and hear what is said about them, and no one who knows

anything at all about it will tell you anything different. But it
did not save either of them from being flung off their perches,
suddenly, ignominiously, humiliatingly, because, in their very
different ways, they failed to negotiate successfully the swirling
political currents which every day surround a London secondary
school head. They fell into the deep, dark pit which operators like
Dibb have managed, so far at least, to avoid. They learned the
hard way that being brilliant at their job was not enough. For both
of them, their peace of mind and their health were destroyed by
the experience.

Both these men have given me, for this book, the first interview
they have given to anyone since the blow fell.

For Smith, the events of April 2006 made him famous,
and brought him to the point where he contemplated suicide.
The massively successful head of All Saints Catholic School
and Technology College in east London, named in 2003 the
second most improved school in England, was invited to join the
council of the Specialist Schools and Academies Trust (SSAT).
This near-quango was set up in 2005 to seek out donors for the
government's city academies programme and was led by Sir Cyril
Taylor, a millionaire businessman, and Tony Blair's chief fundraiser
and close friend Lord Levy. Smith was to help the SSAT to seek
new academy sponsors and help them to set up academies.

The SSAT was investigated by the *Sunday Times* over
allegations that peerages were being offered in exchange for
donations. A reporter posing as the PR assistant of a potential
sponsor recorded Smith making a connection between providing
funding and getting an honour. He allegedly told her: 'The Prime
Minister's office would recommend someone like [the donor]
for an OBE, a CBE or a knighthood.' Investing in five academies
would almost certainly guarantee a peerage, he said. His
indiscretions were splashed all over the newspaper that Sunday.

Of course he was instantly disowned by Taylor and the SSAT,
with the result that they survived, but Smith did not. He was
arrested under the 1925 Honours (Prevention of Abuses) Act as
part of a wider police probe into alleged corruption – the first of

several arrests which came closer and closer to the Prime Minister. Eventually the Crown Prosecution Service announced that he would not face charges, as it had 'insufficient evidence'.

So Smith did not go to jail, as at one point he feared he might. But his distinguished teaching career collapsed in ruins, because he was drawn into politics. His marriage disintegrated, he moved home, he contemplated suicide, and he went to live at a secret address to avoid reporters. Instead of the plaudits which should have greeted his retirement, he crept out of the school for which he had done so much with his tail between his legs.

Paul Patrick, meanwhile, was a stunningly successful head, and had the love and gratitude of the children, staff and parents at Cardinal Wiseman School in west London. The school website trumpets a 'track record of outstanding achievement' starting in September 1997 when 'a new Head teacher, Mr Patrick, arrives'. In 1998 and 1999 the school's GCSE results were the best it had ever known. In 1999 it was named the second most improved school in London by the *Times Educational Supplement* and one of the country's best technology schools by the Technology Colleges Trust. The next year Ofsted called it 'outstanding'. And so on, pages of it – you can read it all in Patrick's profile in this book – right up to another 'outstanding' from Ofsted in 2008 and one from the Roman Catholic Diocese of Westminster this year.

What the website doesn't tell you is that Patrick hasn't been allowed into the school since March 2009. He is barred from speaking to anyone associated with it, and no one wants to talk about him. Patrick arrived home from Cuba – one of his unconventional, but apparently massively successful, innovations is a link with a secondary school in Havana – to receive telephone calls from the governors and the Roman Catholic Diocese of Westminster to say that he was not allowed to come into the school or to contact anyone associated with the school, pending a financial investigation. There were suspicions about the uses to which he had put the money for the Cuban exchange, apparently.

A month later, at seven o'clock one morning, a posse of policemen, some of them from the Fraud Squad, arrived at

Patrick's home, searched it thoroughly and took him to the police station. After several months the police announced there would be no charges, but as I write in January 2010, Patrick has just resigned. The police having found no grounds for prosecution, the school and the diocese mounted their own investigation. Patrick denies any wrongdoing.

So being a rebel helps, but isn't necessary. The same applies to showmanship. Liking children, on the other hand, is vital, and so is some measure of political skill.

And what else?

Phil Cross has been working on a doctorate on how heads should turn round failing schools, which he intends for publication. He concludes that there are a few essentials:

1. Leadership training for head teachers of challenging schools should be more context focused rather than the current 'one size fits all' National Professional Qualification for Headship. Serious thought should be given to a two-year probationary period for new head teachers.
2. Investigate a wider range of credible measures of effectiveness in challenging urban schools serving disadvantaged communities.
3. Step up efforts to define a new paradigm for challenging urban schools that moves us on from the current debate between school effectiveness and school improvement.
4. Test the school improvement model, based on twenty-two statistically derived school improvement factors identified in the research, in a range of other contexts.

Cross believes you treat a failing school differently. When it ceases to be a failing school, it no longer needs special treatment. Teacher and writer Francis Gilbert knew a head who did just that, and he wrote about him in the *Daily Telegraph* on 24 February 2009. He recalled being a teacher at the school from hell: 'Just walking down the corridor was hazardous. Frequently, children would rush up behind me and hit me on the back of the head, shouting out, "Gilly, Gilly, how are ya doing, mate?"' When he complained, his head of year said he needed to get a sense of humour. He recalled lessons where all the pupils pushed the furniture out of the classroom and lit cigarettes; he recalled sitting on a chair which had been booby trapped with ripped-up cans, cutting his backside. And he could not get another job – because no one wanted to employ a teacher from that dreadful school. 'Poor, weak leadership had led to the school gaining very poor results, which had led to the demoralisation of the staff who couldn't leave, which led to even worse teaching.'

Gilbert did get a job etlsewhere eventually, and shortly after, the head was sacked and a new man took over who was 'obsessed with imposing good discipline and getting the children to work hard. He walks around the school with a loudspeaker and fusses endlessly over the state of the pupils' uniform. He and his management team check in on lessons all the time, yanking out miscreants if they step out of line.' Now pupils 'line up quietly for lunch; instead of desperate teachers yelling for order, there is a studious hush in lessons; instead of books being flung around the head of a depressed librarian, there is silent working among the bookshelves. Results have sky-rocketed.'

Gilbert says that even the best teachers flounder when there is no law and order, which is where head teachers come in. 'Great head teachers', he says, 'are old-fashioned creatures. Like Dixon of Dock Green, they patrol their patch religiously, learning the names of every pupil, making sure that the naughty kids are punished and the good ones are praised.' Bad heads are

> glorified bureaucrats: sycophantic managerialists who are obsessed with implementing every government initiative and ingratiating themselves with the educational establishment. They spend too much time at conferences and rarely poke their heads out of their offices when they are at school. Instead, they issue diktats and set up complex reporting and monitoring structures in school that tie up the teachers in paperwork. The name of the game is making sure that they are never blamed for anything and that they gain a great

job after they leave their school – they rarely stay in charge of a school more than five years before moving on to the next sinecure.

They are obsessed with data, putting facts and figures above people. They manipulate the curriculum to get good results: this might include encouraging pupils to take soft options, including syllabi stuffed with easy coursework assignments and implementing vocational courses that are impossible to fail.

The taste and texture of effective school leadership

For heads themselves, and those teachers who want to become heads; for school governors who have to appoint heads; and for parents who have to choose schools for their children – at least partly on what they think of the head – this book is fundamentally different from what's already available, and performs a different function.

They already have access to statistical surveys showing that this or that method produces this or that improvement in results, and MBA-type studies of leadership. They already have the research and training provided by the National College for Leadership of Schools and Children's Services. There was a time when teachers just worked their way up to become heads. Today this progression is professionalised, and all head teachers have to have a qualification in school leadership from the National College. This does at least mean that they are trained in the required skills, though the fear has to be that the process will start to weed out mavericks like David Nichols, Paul Kelley, Phil Cross and Sue Seifert.

Seifert, who of course became a head teacher long before such things were required, had to advise her eventual successor, Nick Tait, on the application process for this course, which (naturally) requires you to fill in a very, very long form. In an interview later published by the National College, Tait said:

The initial application form took me a long time to complete
– at least twenty hours, I'd say, spread over several Sunday
afternoons. The way it was structured really helped, though,
because the form was sectioned according to the various
different areas of headship. That meant I could do a chunk,
then go away, reflect, get some advice and guidance from my
head teacher and colleagues and come back to it another day to
improve on what I'd written.

Then there's a two-day assessment. Tait loved it:

It was hard work and very intensive – but brilliant to
have two days focused purely on you. The one-to-one sessions
with the assessors, the mock interviews – so, so rewarding
and useful, and great practice for when you come to do your
real-life headship interviews. There's about one assessor for
every two people, so you really are watched quite intensively
and they pick up on so much about you and your style of
leadership – things you'd never have noticed in yourself
before.

The National College produces a considerable amount of
research and tries to identify the most important skills. Recently
it has been emphasising the importance of emotional intelligence
(EI), a bit of jargon that crept into several of my interviews.
A 2009 research paper by Kevin Bullock, head teacher of Fordham
Church of England Primary School in Cambridgeshire, called
*The Importance of Emotional Intelligence to Effective School
Leadership*, offers a good deal of abstract information. In it
Bullock wrote:

73 per cent of head teachers rated EI as 'very important' –
markedly higher than for senior managers (61 per cent). Men
were slightly more likely to view EI in these terms, with 76
per cent stating it was 'very important' compared with 71 per
cent of their female colleagues.

Aspects of EI which were viewed as particularly important centred on being able to:

> rise above personal differences
> bounce back from difficult situations/experiences
> deal with other people's anger effectively and
> spot unrest/anxiety/anger swiftly and
  respond appropriately.

[. . .]

70 per cent of head teachers viewed high expectations as very important, as did 69 per cent of senior managers. Ensuring a clear focus on the organisation's goals, identifying and challenging under-performance and ensuring high standards across the whole organisation were major themes within this, while sharing the vision with others was also critical.

The report concludes with these unsurprising observations: 'Evidence from this study indicates that these senior leaders and headteachers viewed EI as the most important qualities for effective school leadership. However, there is also clear evidence that EI offered no guarantee of success on its own, but rather was highly interdependent on high expectations and effective communication.' What this does not offer is any sense of what it means in practice, of how it actually works; and that is what I have tried to supply here.

How can we help heads to succeed?

Successive governments in the last thirty years have had a tendency to micro-manage schools, encouraging in heads a sort of tick-box mentality. The heads in this book have largely managed to free themselves from it, otherwise they could not be as effective as they are. Whether they despise Ofsted and government circulars, like David Nichols, or quite like them, as Philip Friend does, at least an effective head gets them in proportion. They do not fall into the trap of living for them, as the head in Francis Gilbert's entertaining book *Teacher on the Run* does. Gilbert reports that he drew up action planning worksheets, and none of the teachers or children took the slightest notice:

> Although I was quite dispirited about the poor reception my action planning worksheets had received, I soon got over my depression when I realised that the really important people in the school were hugely impressed by my efforts. The head teacher and the deputy head thought I had done a terrific job. They had been given a target by the governing body to introduce action planning into the sixth form by such and such a date, and they could now tick them off in their review.

They encourage their staff to exercise their own judgement, too. Joanne Dean at St Ives Infant School made it clear to me that she expected her teachers to take what they wanted out of such things as government literacy strategies, and leave the rest. She broke the shackles for her staff, which is one reason why she is effective. It's the only way to deal with shackles, and Gilbert would be pleased to work for her. If you followed the instructions from Whitehall to the letter, you would run your literacy lesson to the second as you were told to run it, and in some schools they do.

In their different styles, the heads in the book deal with government directives in the way advocated by Terry Wrigley, senior education lecturer at Edinburgh University and editor of the journal *Improving Schools*, in his 2006 book *Another School is Possible*. The government, he wrote, had

> turned England's primary schools upside down by insisting that there was only one way to teach reading – the stereotyped literacy hour. Teachers were given a blast of quick-fix training and expected to obediently deliver the set pattern. Their existing expertise was ignored – though fortunately many were bold enough to adapt the literacy hour according to their professional judgement.

The same point was made to me about twenty years ago by Professor Marie Clay, the New Zealand educationalist who developed reading recovery. Reading recovery is the only means yet found to get children reading who have been unable to learn the skill, and in the last years of John Major's Conservative government, the Labour Party promised to import it to Britain, though, unsurprisingly, in government they found it too expensive and introduced the literacy hour instead.

Clay told me that the trouble with British primary education is that we had allowed the two sides in educational arguments to become two armed camps, which they had managed to avoid in New Zealand. In Britain you either believed in teaching children to read by using phonics, in which case the left damned you as a 1950s-style authoritarian; or you believed in teaching them to read by using real books, in which case the right called you a 1960s hippie and demanded you revert to type and arrive at school in a beard, sandals and multi-coloured sweater. In New Zealand, she said, teachers knew you needed both phonics and real books, and struck their own balance between them.

Effective heads understand that ideas about how to teach are just that – ideas. They are not holy writ. And when they cease to understand that, they become tickers of boxes, not head teachers. Francis Gilbert described the process with deadly accuracy in his 2005 book *Teacher on the Run*. Under the heading 'How to generate lots of useless bits of paper that get thrown in the bin' he describes the process of action planning. 'First you ask that every student becomes an action planner. Then you ask a very junior member of staff, who has inadvertently alienated just about everyone, who knows nothing about action planning, and who has no training in the field, to introduce action planning.' And so on. Gilbert describes his own attempt, on instructions, to introduce 'action planning' in the sixth form, in which students would set themselves realistic targets – that is, apparently, targets which were SMART – Specific, Measurable, Achievable, Realistic and Time-related. (No head who is any good relies on these dreadful little acronyms, which are really an excuse for not thinking seriously about anything.)

The trouble with many of the students' action plans, Gilbert found, was that they set the target of raising their grades without adding any specific action they could take to achieve this target. But, he found, it did not matter.

It takes a very brave head to ignore all the silly targets, forget about ticking boxes and get on with the job. That's part of the reason why so many of the heads in this book are natural rebels. A head who does defy the tick-box culture had better make pretty sure his results are good, too, otherwise they'll have him. And sometimes even that's not good enough, as Paul Patrick found out.

Oddly, out of the heads in this book, the successful heads whom I identified myself or from my contacts – for example Phil Cross and David Nicholls – were more likely to be rebels than those I first went to because they had been named Head Teacher of the Year, such as Kevin Harcombe or Jo Shuter. Whether this tells us something about the way head teachers of the year are chosen, or something about me and the people I talk to, I have no idea.

But I am quite clear that the rebels are preferable to the heads who feel the need obediently to festoon their notepaper with logos – a member of the Specialist Schools and Academies Trust, a technology college, a specialist school, all the New Labour stamps of approval. Cross told me his notepaper looked almost indecently naked beside that of his colleagues, but he did not mind because he knew his school and his pupils were succeeding. It is all just a way of changing the name and the appearance of something, in the vain hope that this will change the substance.

Once, most children were educated at places called schools. Only the very rich went to colleges, with names like Eton College, and they paid through the nose. During the 1970s, the word 'school' started to mean 'terrifying concrete jungle filled with drug-crazed teenagers where teachers dare not tread', so when Margaret Thatcher's education secretary Kenneth Baker invented a new sort of school, to be handed over to private companies, he called them, not schools, but colleges. Thus was born the city technology college.

The trouble with verbal gentrification is that it needs constantly to reinvent itself. Within a few years, 'college' came to mean 'terrifying concrete jungle filled with drug-crazed teenagers where teachers dare not tread'. So when New Labour decided to relaunch city technology colleges, it needed a new name. Enter city academies, now just academies.

In a few years from now, 'academy' will mean 'terrifying concrete jungle filled with drug-crazed teenagers where teachers dare not tread', but I suspect our politicians are ahead of the game. In the splendid Westminster offices occupied by the Department of Children, Schools and Families there is, I am sure, a sealed envelope marked 'to be opened by the education secretary after academies have failed'. And inside it, the secretary of state of the day will find one word: 'conservatoire'. You read it here first.

Verbal gentrification goes back to the birth of universal state education. The 1945 government decided there should be two sorts of secondary school. There were to be grammar schools for brainy kids, who would grow up to be middle managers and professionals – not quite as grand as those who went to fee-charging schools and were destined to run the country, but fit to be spoken to. The other schools, serving the majority, were for thick kids, destined to be at the bottom of the heap. (Actually, there was a third sort, a compromise between the two, but they never caught on and need not detain us here.) But 'schools for thick kids, destined to be at the bottom of the heap' was not the way to sell them. Ministers had the brilliant idea of calling them 'secondary moderns'. Then as now, the word 'modern' was thought of as making anything attractive. But, horrifyingly fast, the words 'secondary modern' came to mean 'school for thick kids, destined to be at the bottom of the heap'.

Frantic efforts were made to save the words. Teachers and education administrators were instructed to say that you did not 'pass' or 'fail' the eleven-plus exam, which decided whether you went to a grammar or a secondary modern; you were just selected for 'a different type of school'. Parents and children knew they were being lied to. So Harold Wilson's education secretary Anthony Crosland started abolishing the eleven-plus and secondary moderns. Because the Wilson government disliked top-down solutions and wanted some local autonomy (how absurdly fastidious that seems now), the job was not complete when Labour lost office in 1979 and secondary moderns had a new lease of life.

But their name had to be gentrified. There are almost no schools left which call themselves secondary moderns. In those parts of the country that still operate the eleven-plus, such as Kent, secondary moderns are generally called 'high schools'. It must have struck someone in government as pleasing to call the lowest of the low 'high schools' – like Orwell's Ministry of Truth, which told lies, and his Ministry of Peace, which made war. And now the inevitable is happening. 'High school' is generally understood to mean 'school for thick kids, destined to be at the bottom of the heap'. Soon a new name will be needed, and I have a small bet on 'new technological conservatoires'.

I think all the heads in this book know that changing the name achieves nothing, and we can help them by stopping the politicians from pretending that it does.

We can also help them with a move to more ethnic minority heads. The 2009 report on the state of the labour market for senior school staff prepared for the National Association of Head Teachers (NAHT) and the Association of School and College Leaders (ASCL) by Professor John Howson says:

> Teachers from minority groups still comprise a very small percentage of those appointed to leadership positions, and this remains an area of concern for those responsible for succession planning at all levels including below the leadership scales . . .
>
> Senior appointments remain overwhelmingly from the white community. This year [2009] 540 of the 556 appointments were described as white compared with three mixed, nine Asian/Asian British, three Black/Black British and one Chinese/other ethnic group. This means that there were sixteen appointments of non-white head teachers recorded.

This is an improvement on the eight recorded last year, but still accounts for just less than 3 per cent of recorded appointments.

As it happens, in this collection of interviews there are no heads from ethnic minorities, and when I realised this, I did wonder briefly whether I ought not to go out and interview one. An obvious candidate might have been Sir William Atkinson at Phoenix High School in west London. But that, surely, would be an insult to the estimable Sir William, whose record speaks for itself, or to any other head whom I might approach in order to provide ethnic balance.

However, it is worth asking why there are so few, and Howson suggests one possible contributory cause: 'There appear to be significant age points after which progression to a more senior post becomes considerably more difficult. Whether these barriers discriminate against certain groups, including those taking a career break, and later entrants to the profession, is worthy of further consideration.'

There seems to be a reluctance to appoint either those near the start of their careers, or those near the end, to headships, according to Howson, and this may help to explain why there are fewer women heads than their numbers in the teaching profession suggest there ought to be. Howson notes:

Although women are appointed to the majority of primary headships, they are still under-represented in respect of their overall percentage of the workforce. The same is true in the secondary sector, even though on the limited evidence of the schools who responded to this survey, more women are now being appointed to secondary headships.

*

As I put the finishing touches to this book, I hit a depressing watershed. I always ask to be shown round schools by pupils.

At the very last one I went to, for the very first time, the head said: 'I'm so sorry, but are you CRB [Criminal Records Bureau] checked?'

I'm not. Recent events mean that I must be. There are frightening rumours among heads. One says that Ofsted was about a give a school an outstanding verdict, until one of the inspectors pointed out that the head had not asked, when they arrived, whether they were CRB checked; and on those grounds, they failed the school. Whether the story is exactly true does not matter. The fact that heads believe it is what matters.

If I were to do any more of these profiles, I would have to get CRB checked first. It seems a good time to stop.

Phil Cross
The head as campaigner

Originally published 13 September 2007

In his first year as head at Hurlingham and Chelsea School,
in the London Borough of Hammersmith and Fulham, Phil Cross
got it out of special measures. In his second year, he set it on a path
of steeply rising exam results. In his third, he fought off a proposal
to close the school. I rolled up on the first day of his fourth year.
He had just taken delivery of a report which, for the first time
since he took over, seemed to guarantee the school a future.

At 8.15 Cross was already on the gate, with a couple of
colleagues, greeting new children and their parents, joking with
older ones, but most of all, casting a critical eye over uniforms,
pulling up ties and warning that lurid trainers would not pass
muster tomorrow. Do uniforms really matter, I asked him? 'All
the time the battle is about the uniform, it's not about something
else,' he said. 'It's the front line.' That illustrates Cross's attitude to
digging schools out of trouble. If he took over a school which was
already running smoothly, he might not worry about uniforms.
'You do different things in a school like this from what you'd do
in an already high-performing school.'

Here's another example. 'You get them all, in their uniforms,
in the classroom, the teacher starts work, and thirty hands go
up. "Sir, I haven't got a pen." So we provided biros. Why have an
argument over a pen that costs 10 pence? Now we will move to
saying "Bring them in".'

Digging schools out of trouble is Cross's main interest – he's
doing a doctorate in it at Greenwich University. But he's not

one of those superheads parachuted in at great expense as part
of a package which generally also includes getting rid of the
local authority, clearing out half the staff, going for trust or
academy status, excluding dozens of pupils and persuading some
big company to allow its logo to be displayed in the entrance.
He's almost the reverse. 'I came in through the old Inner London
Education Authority. I'm for mixed-ability comprehensive schools,
the planning powers of the local authority.'

The school's progress under his leadership has been remarkable.
In 2004 just one in five children got five A*–Cs at GCSE. It was
nearly one in three the next year, more than one in three in 2006,
and in 2007 it was more than half. The school is a quieter, more
peaceful place. Fights and bullying are rare instead of being the
norm, corridors are virtually empty during lessons, most pupils
arrive on time and, according to a teacher who has been there for
twenty-seven years, 'we're no longer running to stand still'.

Still, you have to run quite often if you want to keep up with
Cross as he walks round his school, even though he stops several
times in each corridor to talk to a pupil or a teacher. He's a
workaholic of forty-nine with greying hair and a light but clipped
voice who misses little. As he route-marched me to the hall he met
a teacher and said: 'There's a little lass new today who was crying
– she doesn't speak much English, she's got glasses and I think
she's from eastern Europe – go into the tutor groups and find her,
make sure she's OK.'

In the hall, he speaks to a whole-school assembly, with a graph
showing the rise in GCSE results beside him. There was an orderly
procession into the hall – 600 pupils aged eleven to sixteen (he's
got no sixth form) – and before he started speaking, you could
hear a pin drop. Three years ago, he says, that speech would have
been hard work. His voice is even, but urgent, and the words are
brisk and to the point. 'Two years ago we came out of special
measures. That's what happens when a school gets into trouble
and you have lots of inspectors in, checking the teachers, checking
you lot. Then last year most of you were very much involved in
a fight for the future of the school.'

Yet the school is doing well, he says, pointing to the graph. 'It shows the improvement. You know the five A*–C that I keep talking to you about? It's a passport to a good job. Look at the improvement we've had over the past few years. Even despite last year, us having to fight for the future of our school, yet it still went up from 34 per cent to 51 per cent. If this doesn't happen I get the sack. But also each of these percentage points represents one and a half children. That's forty or fifty children whose life chances are dramatically improved.'

Then he lists ten points which he claims to have stolen from England rugby coach Clive Woodward, though personally I'm not at all sure he didn't make them up himself. A famous sportsman's ideas are always more interesting than the boring old head teacher's. I am not sure Woodward has ever delivered a homily on attendance, for example, but here's Cross's: 'All those who got five A*–C had an attendance rate of over 90 per cent. The converse was also true. It's a no-brainer, ladies and gentlemen. Some people thought if they were on time four days out of five, that's all right. But if you are late once a week you are already below the 90 per cent.' Another is uniforms: 'If a teacher came here for an interview with a short fat tie and trousers down here somewhere, would I give them a job? No, and you and your parents wouldn't expect me to.'

Then there's the way you speak to people. Cross expects respect from pupils – but he expects his staff to treat them with respect too. 'I had a training day with all the teachers on Monday and one of the things we talked about was teaching children with respect. It's a two-way process. Being in school is a bit like being in work.' He sums up: 'If you do those ten things I can guarantee you will be very successful. If you don't do those ten things you will not be successful. That's quite a good deal, if you think about it.'

Finally he springs a small surprise. Three years ago he introduced student planners, to let the students plan their work and as a way of communicating between teachers and parents. Some children said the planner was too big for their pockets, and that was why they did not use them properly. So he made them half the size. Now 'they will fit neatly in your blazer pocket so there is no excuse for you not to have a planner 24/7'.

Hurlingham and Chelsea has a very mixed intake, both in class and race, with many children crossing the Thames from the poorer parts of Wandsworth to come to it. Cross wants 'to break the link between [the pupils'] social circumstances and their future' and is willing to jettison any activity which does not help to do that: 'If it doesn't impact on children's learning, don't do it.' So is he hampered by the bane of the modern head's life – bureaucracy and paperwork? Surprisingly, he says no. He says that the Department for Children, Schools and Families does not have a lot of police running around to make sure forms are filled in, and I get the strong impression (but he did not say this) that an awful lot of questionnaires rapidly find their way to his bin.

He's very demanding of his staff. 'I want teachers who love working with children. We can sort out the rest. But if you don't like children this job must be horrible.'

In September 2006, having watched him turn the place round and supported him with £600,000 worth of building and equipment, Hammersmith and Fulham Council told Cross that his school was to be closed. For a head who believes in the planning power of the local authority, it came as a nasty shock, especially since there was no proper plan – the council just expected other schools to absorb its children.

He knew at once that he had to fight it. 'Even if I'd not won the right to keep the school open, the only way I could run the school was to have the fight,' he says.

The decision was made partly because, as often happens when a school goes into special measures, the number of applicants went down. The relatively affluent families living near the school stopped sending their children there, and more children came from further afield – often south of the river and outside Hammersmith and Fulham. There are two voluntary aided schools in the borough – one is the London Oratory, to which Tony Blair sent his children from faraway Islington – and Cross thinks the council wanted more schools like those. The council's decision led some of his governors to think about getting out of local authority control, but Cross talked them out of that approach.

He involved children and their parents from the start, and produced a detailed document called *The Case for a Future for Hurlingham and Chelsea School*. The council said there were enough surplus places in the borough for his 600 children, but he pointed out that the nearest mixed school was in the north of the borough, and he was in the south. The council said that local parents did not want to send their children to his school. So he invited local parents in, to see for themselves that it was no longer the failing, anarchic place they thought it was, and some of them became his firm supporters. Hundreds of people turned up to Save Hurlingham and Chelsea School meetings, and in April 2007 the councillors reversed their decision. Hurlingham and Chelsea was reprieved, and there was to be a commission under Baroness Perry of Southwark on schools organisation in that part of the borough.

That commission reported last week. The school, it said, should stay open and should get a sixth form – and, if possible, work in partnership with another school, perhaps the new lycée which the French government may decide to build in the borough. Cross is likely to welcome a genuine partnership with another school, though there would probably be another battle if it looked like a takeover, as in the academy model. 'This report indicates a strong future for us,' he says. 'We have to build, but not to destabilise what we have. We don't want any more battles.'

Update

Shortly after I visited, Ofsted came to call, and in January 2008 concluded:

> Hurlingham and Chelsea is a good and rapidly improving school with outstanding features. The staff are passionate about school improvement and are successfully focused on placing the quality of teaching and learning at its heart. As a

result, standards have improved rapidly from a very low base three years ago. In 2007, 41 per cent of students achieved 5+ A*–C grades, including English and mathematics. The school was recently named as the most improved secondary school in London for sustained improvement in GCSE results between 2004 and 2007, and the second most improved school nationally. Students of all abilities are valued equally and make good progress. Particularly strong and consistent achievement is evident in Years 10 and 11, with the school in the top 2 per cent nationally in 2007. Teaching and learning is good . . . The school is particularly successful in meeting its stated aim of 'breaking the link between social disadvantage and student achievement'.

Breaking that link is still Phil Cross's passion. With those sorts of results, he can hold the politics at bay, and there are no current threats to his school. The idea of linking the school with a new Lycée Français receded, and Cross was quite glad to see the back of it. This brought about a period of relative calm and stability for the school, which has allowed the staff to focus all their efforts on educating children, and he's been promised a sixth form sometime in the next couple of years. 'It's a simple formula: high expectations, good quality staff, treating children with respect.'

The political threats over a long period of time galvanised staff, students and parents in support of the school. Cross is proud of the fact that he has proved at Hurlingham and Chelsea that rapid school improvement does not necessarily require structural changes from the outside such as academies, trusts and specialist status. He is still far from convinced that any of these have a place in school improvement.

He is prepared to consider specialist status in mathematics and ICT, but only as a necessity in order to get funding from the Building Schools for the Future initiative. 'It's the least I can get away with,' he says – the shortest distance he can travel along the New Labour tramline. Left to himself, he'd simply adopt the old sneer about 'bog standard comprehensives' as a badge of honour, and wear it with pride.

Phil Cross has finished his doctorate on how to transform schools like Hurlingham and Chelsea against the odds. His work was based mainly on the perceptions of children, and he's hoping to turn it into a book.

Paul Kelley
The head as rebel

Originally published 18 October 2007

'Where's the head teacher's office?' I asked. We were standing
in the middle of a big, glass-ceilinged space which they call the
Pyramid, filled with banks of computers and shelves of books, and
thronged with students. 'He's over there,' said my guide, pointing
to a tall, slim, grey-haired man working at one of the desks.

'No, I don't have an office,' Paul Kelley tells me in that dark,
slow, meaningful voice I always associate with Californian radicals
who are old enough to have marched against the Vietnam war,
which is exactly what he is.

Not having an office started out, as many things do at
Monkseaton High School, in North Tyneside, as a response to
a cramped, inadequate early 1970s building, in which only the
Pyramid – added in 1996 on Kelley's watch – does not regularly
flood. But Kelley discovered he liked working where everyone
could see him, and the pupils I spoke to seem to like it as well.
So when the school gets its new building – in May 2009 if all goes
according to plan – there will still be no head teacher's office.

The staff room, like the head who sits just outside it, is highly
visible. You can see everything that goes on there through the
windows of the Pyramid. So no one bothers to look. They know
that the sight of a teacher drinking tea is terminally tedious.

Paul Kelley will probably always be remembered as the Laura
Spence head. In 1999, Laura, one of his sixth-formers, was
predicted to get the best possible A-levels (and did get them), was
accepted by top universities all over the world and was offered a

scholarship at Harvard – but she was turned down by Magdalen College, Oxford. A tutor's notes said she might not fit in because she lacked confidence, 'as with other comprehensive school pupils'. Kelley says she did not lack confidence, and was talented and funny as well as academically brilliant.

The then Chancellor, Gordon Brown, called the Oxford decision a disgrace, to the private fury of Prime Minister Tony Blair, who had got his Oxford place from a splendid public school with comparatively indifferent A-levels. Kelley insists this had nothing to do with him: he has never spoken to Brown or any of his aides.

The Oxford establishment was furious. The week I visited the school, Dr David Starkey was still insisting, as Magdalen did at the time, that Oxford continues to take half its pupils from the 7 per cent of the population who attend fee-charging schools because comprehensive school teachers discourage their pupils from applying. The charge made by the dons is that comprehensive schools tell their pupils they will feel out of place in Oxford.

In twenty years of writing about education, I have met dozens of comprehensive school teachers, every one of whom would encourage any pupil who seemed to have a chance of an Oxbridge place. So I am inclined to side with Kelley when he says the dons are talking rubbish: 'They keep saying everything is all right and it is all someone else's fault. That's a bit sad. I'm not making a personal attack on them, just saying that the system got it wrong.' He thinks the system by which Oxbridge colleges are all responsible for selecting their own students ensures they will continue to get it wrong sometimes.

Laura Spence justified her head teacher's confidence. An outstanding athlete as well as a top-class academic, she was the first British woman to row for Harvard, despite never having rowed before she went there. She later returned to Britain to study medicine at Cambridge.

As for Kelley, he's found other ways of making the British establishment foam at the mouth. Last month he irritated the Church of England with his plea to be allowed to run a secular school, free from the ministrations of the local authority's Standing Advisory Council on Religious Education, which tells schools how to teach religion. 'A child has the right to be introduced to all views, including the secular one,' he says. 'It is not the function of schools to promote a particular religious or political belief.' He mentions, deadpan, that the choice is either making education formally secular, as in France and the USA, or formally religious, as in Britain and Iran.

Kelley's plea was turned down, but he still does not hold a Christian assembly, for which Ofsted routinely deducts points from the school's score. He can afford that. Because the trouble with Kelley is that he runs a thoroughly successful school in unpromising circumstances. Before he arrived, no pupil at Monkseaton had gone to any of Britain's top universities; now there's a steady trickle. Laura Spence was his second Harvard scholarship: Laura Dixon won one the previous year. It helped, of course, that their American head knew the US system, but 'every head brings what he's got to the job'.

His exam results are good, and Ofsted praises his school. It feels like a safe, purposeful place; pupils of all ages talked to me with cheerful confidence. The school's intake comes largely from the three council estates which border it – the better-off local families' children go to a school in the better-off part of the town – so, especially with its tatty buildings, it could easily have a secondary modern feel about it, but it doesn't.

Kelley was determined I should not leave until I had inspected his toilets. The innovation he wanted me to notice is devastatingly simple. Each cubicle opens directly onto the corridor. There are no communal areas. At a stroke he has eliminated the smoking and bullying traditionally associated with school toilets.

He is, by any measure, an effective head, so there is not much that ministers and the educational establishment can do about the fact that he is irredeemably off message. He clearly spelled out his heretical views in his book *Making Minds*. (He wanted to call it 'Not Good Enough', but his publisher wisely drew his attention to the fun that unkind reviewers could have with that.)

The book says we should not teach grammar – it does not help anyone to write better English. It says that focusing on examination results and measurable outputs 'reflects a system that has lost its way'. Ofsted is worse than useless, judging schools 'in an antiquated, expensive and inaccurate way'. Politicians 'focus on education and stamp their prejudices (or those of the swing voters) onto it', with the result that 'education has become a multi-million-dollar and largely unaccountable government industry'. He's not impressed by school uniform, and would scrap it 'if I was allowed to by the governors and if it would work in English society'.

So he has to be good. Any slippage of standards will be seized on as proof that this dreadful Californian relic of the liberal 1960s is leading us to hell in a handcart. Yet he's as off message for the left as for the government, for his was the first trust school, with sponsorship from the Open University and Microsoft, both of which have contributed to the innovations he has pioneered at the school. These include an arrangement for seven former pupils who left school at sixteen to work at the school, and be paid, while they complete an Open University degree, and get time off to do so. There is also an initiative in language learning. Convinced that languages should be taught early, Kelley has arranged for his language teachers to go into local primary schools.

His style of teaching is as distinctive as his leadership style. I watched him with a class of fourteen-year-olds. He illustrated his message about healthy eating with his own diet, which has enabled him to lose a stone in the past year. It's no joke. I had lunch with him afterwards. His lunch was a strong black coffee – not healthy, maybe, but certainly slimming. He showed them his screensaver – a picture of his own four grown-up children – and promised that next time he would tell them what the youngest, Nancy, is doing right now in Canada, and about her adventures in a Canadian forest. He broke up the session with the most brutal game of Simon Says that I've seen. I was the first to make a mistake and drop out; everyone else was used to the unforgiving rules.

Kelley has a lifetime's experience of getting up the noses of the establishment. That's how he comes to be in Britain. In 1964 he spent several nights in Californian jails. Every time they let him out, he went straight back to the occupation of the Sheraton Palace Hotel in San Francisco, which was refusing to employ anyone from an ethnic minority in any job which involved meeting customers.

In 1968 he left the land of his birth forever. With a Chinese stepmother, racist graffiti would be scrawled on the walls of his family home, and young men like him were being forced to go and fight people like his stepmother in Vietnam. He was excused the draft on health grounds, but would certainly have refused to go anyway. To him, 'the Americans were the invaders and the South Vietnam government were the collaborators'. Now aged nearly sixty and with thirteen years as a head teacher behind him, Paul Kelley still hasn't learned to mince his words.

Update

Paul Kelley still has no office. These days, he doesn't even have a set place to work – you can find him hunched over a desk or a table pretty well anywhere in the school. But he does have a magnificent new building, of which he is very proud. After it had been open for three weeks, in October 2009, he told me:

> It has very high natural light. It controls temperature, CO_2 levels and moisture to 'natural levels', has no square rooms, and only triangular or round tables. But mainly, it is a beautiful and innovative space. Visitors keep saying how quiet and calm it is.

The school's results still keep the wolves at bay. The proportion of pupils who get five GCSEs at A*–C has increased every year for the last five years, and now stands at 51 per cent. Sixth-form results are improved too. Laura Spence and Laura Dixon were the first of many to go the USA: each year for the past five years, at least one has followed them.

At sixty-one, he has no plans at all to retire. He'd like to go on until he's sixty-five, and longer still if he's allowed to – but assuming he has to go when he's sixty-five, he's open to offers, he says.

And Laura Spence? She graduated from Cambridge with a distinction and is now a doctor with a 30 per cent research remit. She represented Harvard at rowing and Cambridge in running. And she went back to the school on 6 November 2009 to make a speech at the formal opening of the new building. Gordon Brown wasn't invited, apparently.

Kevin Harcombe
The head as busker

Originally published 8 November 2007

It took me a while to realise the primary school assembly had started. No one called for silence, much less bawled out a child for continuing to talk. But slowly I became aware that Kevin Harcombe, the head teacher, was playing the piano at the front of the room. Then the whole school started to sing:

> I will bring to you the best gift I can offer;
> I will sing to you the best things in my mind.

After a couple of verses, the back projection on the big screen behind him shifted, and the movement became a shred jerky, which is when I noticed two children at the front, efficiently making sure the words on the screen kept pace with those being sung.

Then Harcombe handed out some awards: to this small child for wizardry in learning his three times table, to that slightly larger one for learning her eight times. Parents of every child getting an award have been asked to come. If they can't come today, the award is put off until next week. Harcombe thinks it's very important that they should be there to see it. He makes sure every child gets at least two awards during the year.

Next he picked up his guitar. After a couple of chords the pupils knew what was coming, even though they must find the words puzzling:

There's a blaze of light in every word;
It doesn't matter what you heard;
The holy, or the broken Hallelujah.

Some more awards followed, including the winner of the head's award for improved work and behaviour. Then came a very difficult song, sung to Harcombe's guitar and made even harder by his insistence that one half of the room had to sing the first few words of a line, and the other half the rest of it. Next was a special award, suggested by a class teacher, to a little boy who bounded to the front to receive it, 'for being a pleasure to teach and for working his socks off'. One more song, and the school left to a recording of Johann Strauss's *Radetzky March*, a stirring tune with a heavy beat. Some children threw their shoulders back and marched ostentatiously to the music. Most were smiling. It was a pretty good start to their working day.

As they left, two older pupils were writing up the revised house points Harcombe had announced. It all looked cheerful and purposeful. 'Makes you feel good all day, doesn't it?' said one of the parents as he felt in his pocket for his car keys.

Sadly, I wasn't there on a day when a teacher was going on maternity leave, or when there was some other excuse to talk about babies. That, I heard in the staff room, is something the children look forward to, because it allows Harcombe to bring out his party piece, the 'Nappy Calypso'. This is a song about potty training (which Harcombe can only dimly remember – his own three children are now seventeen, fifteen and twelve), written by two teacher friends of his.

I was in my room the other day.
My mummy said she had a game to play.
She stole my nappy and began to sing
And made me sit down on this freezing plastic thing.

After that it becomes scatological.

The Friday morning assembly at Redlands Primary School in Fareham, Hampshire, is a one-man virtuoso performance, from someone who is used to playing difficult audiences. Harcombe helped pay for his BA course in English literature and then his Master's in English Renaissance literature, both at Sussex University, by busking in the streets of Brighton, playing the guitar while a friend played the fiddle. First they played the songs that would get in the money. In those days, at the end of the 1970s, their number one crowd pleaser was 'Mull of Kintyre'. 'People went dewy eyed and threw us silver. When we had enough money, we'd play what we wanted: Stéphane Grappelli, Django Reinhardt.'

Their first school audience was at Roedean, the top girls' public school near Brighton. A Roedean teacher heard them in Brighton's Churchill Square (always a more profitable venue than the Lanes, apparently) and asked them to come to the school and sing, for £5 and as much beer as they could carry away.

When Harcombe graduated, he was not thinking of being a teacher. It was the start of the 1980s, when a sad joke did the rounds: 'What do you say to a literature graduate with a job? – "Big Mac and chips, please."' He was on the dole, then did clerical jobs for the civil service – he was a tax inspector for a while. In 1985, aged twenty-eight, he was back at Sussex for a teaching certificate. At first he was unsure about this new career, but he was quickly enthused, first by an inspirational tutor at Sussex, Neville West, and then by his placement in a Brighton primary school. Armed with certificates, he and his partner – also a newly qualified teacher – started to look for jobs in the same part of the country, and Hampshire was the first to offer them both work.

Quite soon he found himself participating in the 1987 national teachers' strike, and the experience rather blunted the political radicalism of the Sussex University graduate with the instinctive union solidarity of working-class Liverpool.

As a newly qualified teacher, my salary was so meagre I had to supplement it by teaching guitar after school. Moral courage

duly screwed to the sticking place, I informed my head, a
true-blue Tory gent, that I would be withdrawing my labour
in solidarity with my union brothers and sisters. Sadly, when it
came to the big day, solidarity, like Elvis, had left the building
and I was the only teacher in my school taking action. I hastily
altered my placards to 'One Out – One Out!' and 'The worker
[singular] united will never be defeated'!

He was left with world-weary cynicism:

To be an effective striker you need public sympathy (like the
nurses) or, alternatively, the public's testicles in your grasp
(like the power workers). Teachers have public sympathy
to an extent, partly because we seldom take industrial
action, but do we have a grip on the nation's testes? Hardly.
A teachers' strike would cause some problems with child
care, but homes would not be plunged into the dark and
cold – bread would still be on the table, petrol in the car. For
parents, it would be irritating (there goes the sympathy), but
not a testicle-crushing moment. For most children it would
simply be an extra holiday.

By 1995 Harcombe was head of a school in Gosport, and he
moved to head Redlands in 2000. It wasn't a failing school, but
it wasn't a particularly successful one either. It had a poor local
reputation: parents tried to get their children into other schools.
Inspectors called it 'satisfactory' with 'significant weaknesses'
– now they call it 'outstanding'. As Hampshire goes, it is not
in a wealthy area, and one fifth of the children are eligible for
free school meals. But 'I wanted to be head of this school,'
said Harcombe. 'It had a nice feel to it. There's a real sense of
community round here. If you haven't got parents on side, forget
it. I tightened up the teaching, raised expectations among children
and parents. High expectations is the key.'
    Brought up in Liverpool, with no tradition of education in
his own family, he was inspired by his primary school teachers,

and wants to do the same for his pupils. 'I want people to be able to say afterwards that their school encouraged them.' He's also instinctively democratic and egalitarian. All staff – not just the teachers – can attend his senior management meetings, and every child gets a personally signed Christmas card from the head.

Redlands is winning back the pupils who would have gone to neighbouring schools, and Harcombe can take his pick of the local teaching talent because he has a reputation for encouraging and supporting his staff, and giving them what they want. 'We wanted whiteboards and more computer equipment – an investment of £2,000 in every room. We told Kevin, and he found a way to pay for it,' says one. The new computer room, as well as the well-equipped music room, would be the envy of many primary schools.

The staff appreciate that their head wants to develop their skills, likes sending them on courses and makes sure they don't get stale. 'He's a strong head, respectful of children, and brings out the best in children and staff,' says one teacher. They like the fact that he does not take work home, and does not expect them to. He works hard in the school from 8 a.m. to 5.45 p.m. and then goes home. He believes in a proper work–life balance.

They also like the fact that he himself takes on the occasional wearing child with real behavioural problems, and generally manages to do something about him or her. He knows the teacher needs relief from that child sometimes, and the child needs special help and a lot of patience. In the staff room they recalled one boy whom they all dreaded teaching. One day Harcombe tactfully took him away, taught him to play the guitar, and told him how good he was at it. The change in the boy's behaviour was obvious to everyone. Harcombe himself says: 'Sometimes a child comes from another school with a dreadful reputation for behaviour, but he's a pussycat here because we treat him with respect and expect respect back.'

He isn't a so-called superhead, rushing in and clearing out all the old staff – in fact, some of his most valued teachers were there before he was, and he dislikes the superhead concept. Nonetheless, at the age of fifty he was named Primary Head Teacher of the Year in the 2007 Teaching Awards by the National College for School Leadership. His staff were delighted. The children were quite tickled, too. 'Mr Harcombe gets in lots of newspapers and he's won awards,' says Robert, one of four children aged nine and ten who were detailed to show me round.

The award judges talked of his humanity, common sense, humour, optimism, drive, high expectations, trust in his team and unassuming nature. These, they wrote, 'form a unique blend of leadership that is of outstanding quality'. Ofsted said:

> The inspirational head teacher provides effective and determined leadership with a strong focus on raising standards and promoting high standards of care. He is ably supported by a skilled senior management team . . . As a result, the school is an inclusive community where children achieve well. All pupils, including those from minority ethnic groups, those newly arrived and those of different abilities, feel welcomed and want to learn.

'He always has a smile on his face,' says Hannah. She is on the school council, where 'we talk about what we can do better with the school grounds'. There used to be a little hill in the playground, now demolished, and the council is much occupied with the debate about what will replace it, she tells me.

Kayleigh explains about Pupil Voice. Small groups gather with a senior teacher and make suggestions to improve things. They might say that a particular teacher's methods are not working. And changes happen. 'You don't see it at once but you do after a couple of weeks,' says Kayleigh. In the staff room I'm told: 'When we come up with ideas, he gets in behind us.' Maybe that's half the secret of Harcombe's success: when pupils and teachers talk, he listens. And the other half is that when he plays the piano or the guitar, they listen.

Update

Winning Primary Head Teacher of the Year brings rewards. Kevin Harcombe has become one of those heads who get asked to write articles, and comment, and run prestigious seminars, and judge future education awards, and so on. He's been commissioned to write two books – one on how to survive and succeed as a head, another on how to be a brilliant primary school teacher.

So does he still find time to run the school? Absolutely, he says – because he's got good staff round him.

Outside school, his band disbanded, but he's formed another one, which had its first gig in November 2009. He's thought a bit more about what sort of musician he is, and says: 'I like folk music but I've never knowingly put my finger in my ear or worn an Arran sweater.'

If he had to sum up the secret of success in primary schools in one sentence, it would be: 'Love and respect the children but don't indulge them.'

Jo Shuter
The head as heroine

Originally published 6 December 2007

In the reception area at Quintin Kynaston School, there's a prominent picture of Jo Shuter, with a quote from the school's Ofsted report: 'The head teacher's dynamic, keen and determined leadership drives the school forward.' Underneath, there's a quote from 'Jo Shuter, Head Teacher of the Year 2007' about how she adores the job. On another wall, a history of how this handsome reception area came to be built explains that 'the head, Jo Shuter, has done much to give the school a sense of pride and purpose'. Corridor walls carry more pictures of the charismatic Shuter, and there's a newly built coffee bar (sixth-formers and teachers only except on club nights) called Joanna's. It was a school council decision to name it after the head, but she's naturally delighted.

It's the hero head personified. Shuter's style is not for the shrinking violet. But is it all taking the cult of personality too far? Jo Shuter in the flesh is quick and fluent, with an untidy mass of brown, curled hair, a wonderfully mobile face, and a great, deep, dark brown laugh that sounds as though you could be warmed by it from the other side of town. She's instantly charismatic and disarmingly honest, and defuses anything that sounds like criticism by agreeing with it. Yes, she says, there's a cult of personality: 'School success is about leadership. I'm a maverick and a risk taker. The wonderful thing about being a head teacher is that you can do your own thing, and I hope that rubs off on the kids.'

Well, I say querulously, you want them to do their own thing, but you force them into uniforms? A lesser head would tie herself in linguistic knots trying to square the circle, but Shuter blows me away with a gale of laughter: 'Yes, it's double standards, isn't it?' She adds: 'I like all that – no trainers, wear uniforms, line up before going into the classroom, call teachers Sir or Miss. There was a view in some London comprehensives that it stifles creativity. I think that's a load of tosh.'

But the next thing I learn is that she herself was a rebel at school. She was born in 1961 into a north London Jewish family; her father was an accountant and her mother ran a restaurant where, as a teenager, she did some waitressing. She was destined either for the selective grammar school Henrietta Barnett or the private North London Collegiate School, until she deliberately failed her eleven-plus so that she could go to the local comprehensive.

'I was born with a really good brain.' There is no air of boasting, she is just informing me of a fact, and it doesn't occur to me to doubt her. 'So even though I was a rebel, I got really good exam results. Then I wanted to be a PE teacher, because I was really good at PE and it allowed me to burn off energy, but the school said that was a waste and I ought to do law, and I went to Bristol and started a law course and I was bored, bored, bored.' She transferred to social science and psychology, left with a 2:1 and a husband, and went with the latter to Birmingham, where she took a teaching certificate in PE and English.

She came to Quintin Kynaston, in the City of Westminster, in 2002. It's just the sort of inner city school that poses the biggest challenge for a head. Half the pupils are poor enough to qualify for free school meals, which is well above the national average. Many students are resident in areas which are considered economically disadvantaged, and four out of ten of them have learning difficulties or disabilities. Many have statements of special educational needs. Nine out of ten are from ethnic minorities, many of them from refugee or asylum-seeker families. Three quarters speak English as an additional language. And the school was struggling to cope. She decided it was not being firm enough with its pupils.

'There was something of an atmosphere of a seventies London comprehensive about it – no uniforms, children called teachers by their first name.' That wasn't all bad – it meant there was a good relationship between staff and students, and she built on that. She also spent money the school didn't have. 'I went into deficit to buy things. At first I played the baby head: "Oh, sorry, didn't know I was supposed to ask." Then I started getting the local authority to sanction the spending.' The money went on instant improvements to the environment in which children learn, like that spanking new entrance.

Divorced after seventeen years of marriage, she worried about not having time for her own two children. So she gives the best of herself to the school during a long working day, but never takes work home. 'I come in with nothing, I go home with nothing. You hear about heads who shlep all their papers home. I don't do that.' 'Shlep' is a reminder that, though she's lost the religion of her childhood, she's strongly culturally Jewish, certain there's no ailment so serious that a bowl of chicken soup won't cure it.

She does shlep two things home, though: a walkie-talkie and a mobile phone. They go everywhere with her. The walkie-talkie keeps her in touch with everything that happens at QK. The mobile is for Pimlico School.

For, having got QK into the top 3 per cent of schools nationally for value-added student progress, with no permanent exclusions in the last two years, more than 90 per cent attendance and 600 applicants for 210 places, she was asked to do the same for Pimlico, at the other end of Westminster, which went into special measures in January 2007. In 2007 and 2008 she divided her time between the two schools. She used staff expertise from QK at Pimlico, and brought prefects from the two schools together (they asked her which school she cared about more).

There was some resentment at Pimlico – as Shuter says, 'the head can't be everyone's friend'. Many Pimlico parents had great loyalty to the previous head and felt that Westminster City Council had unfairly targeted the school; Shuter was seen as Westminster's instrument for destroying everything that was good about it. She was also seen as an instrument of Westminster's plan to turn Pimlico into an academy. But she did oversee an improvement in Pimlico's results, and she did put up an alternative to the academy route. She and the QK governors put forward a scheme for a federation between the two schools. Each school would have its own head, and she would be in ultimate charge of both of them – which is effectively what happened in 2007 and 2008, when she had a deputy in day-to-day charge of each school.

Pimlico's governors were very keen on the idea. The two schools have a lot in common, and the methods which worked at QK looked set to work at Pimlico. Unfortunately, Westminster Council decided instead to turn Pimlico into an academy, so after this term she will have no further connection with Pimlico. 'I wouldn't choose to be head of an academy,' she says.

She is deeply disappointed. 'Westminster preferred the academy model. I beg to differ. We've made a huge difference at Pimlico. They have their best exam results ever. We were able to mirror the system and structures we have here. I would have loved the opportunity to carry on at Pimlico.' She later clarified this, perhaps after an awkward conversation with Westminster City Council's public relations department, insisting she has 'no axe to grind over academies', and wished to make it clear that she is not opposed to the policies of Westminster City Council.

Even though she is not impressed by academies or trust schools, which makes her very suspect in New Labour circles, she still managed to be one of Tony Blair's favourite heads. When Prime Minister, he visited Quintin Kynaston twice. His famous announcement that he would not serve a full third term was made in QK's playground, and he invited her to breakfast in Downing Street. As he was leaving (to meet President Bush), he put his arm round her and said: 'Lovely to see you, Jo.'

'I don't know why he kept coming here,' she says. 'He picked me, I didn't pick him.' Is she a Blairite on education, I ask. 'I've seen education turned around by the funding that has come in.' That isn't yes or no. I remember how she 'played the baby head' with Westminster Council. She insists that she's not a politician, but she has plenty of political skill.

She's going to need it. She thinks QK will have to become a foundation school as other schools in Westminster become academies. It's on the border of Westminster and Camden, and despite a court ruling some years ago which was thought to make it impossible, Westminster forces her to give priority to children from Westminster primaries – which means that Camden children who live a street or two away might not get in.

She believes firmly in the local community school, taking children who live in the surrounding streets. Two of the most deprived wards in the country are in QK's catchment area. So, too, are some very wealthy homes – some houses in the same street as the school sell for £4½ million – but children from those houses are transported to more distant fee-charging schools. Shuter insists there's nothing that places like the vastly expensive North London Collegiate School – which so narrowly avoided having her education on its conscience – can provide that QK can't.

She wonders aloud whether her popularity in Downing Street was because 'I don't look like a head teacher and New Labour quite likes that'. It's not just the mass of hair and the mobile face, but also a famous tattoo. The day I visited, she wore a black trouser suit which hid it, but rather spoiled the stratagem by owning up to it as soon as I asked. As I left, I said: 'Where's the tattoo exactly?' 'Left ankle,' she shouted. I thought I could still hear her laughing when I got to the Tube station, but perhaps I imagined it.

Update

Quintin Kynaston School broke its link with Westminster City Council to become a foundation school in September 2008 and set itself up as a business, supplying school improvement expertise to local education authorities such as Coventry and Newcastle upon Tyne, and to schools including Westfield Community Technology

College in Watford, in Hertfordshire. It also sells its vocational courses in such subjects as horticulture, construction, and hair and beauty to other schools, and runs profitable conferences on school improvement. And it sells to its old boss, Westminster City Council, places in its new facility for excluded children, which it has created in part of its building.

All this is profitable, and with the money it earns it hires psychiatrists, youth advisers and other professionals it considers essential for its children, but which its state money will not pay for. And it has created an urban farm on its site, which children from inner city tower blocks find fascinating. The farm started with six chickens rescued from battery farms, and now also boasts goats, rabbits and guinea pigs.

Is Shuter turning the place from a school into a business? 'I think that's the way schools have to go nowadays,' she says. Of course, none of it would work if she was shy about blowing her own trumpet, but fortunately shyness is not something from which Shuter suffers. She has a personal state-of-the-art website, with fetching pictures of her carrying off the 2007 Head Teacher of the Year trophy and the sort of quotes a theatre publicist might select from the reviews. For example, Wing Commander Ed Moran (her award was sponsored by the RAF) is quoted as saying:

> Excellence in the teaching profession is crucial to our nation's future and deserves to be recognised. Jo Shuter is an inspirational person who instils in our youth the qualities we so value. She has deservedly risen above the rest and we salute her efforts towards providing our children with the very best start in life.

Then there's a letter from Mike More, chief executive of Westminster City Council:

> Dear Jo, I'm writing to congratulate you on the huge success in taking Pimlico out of special measures. I know that this has taken considerable leadership and sheer hard work. Colleagues

here are delighted and appreciative. Quintin Kynaston is
an outstanding school and exceptionally well led by its
inspirational head teacher. Her powerful, inclusive vision is
shared by all staff and implemented very effectively by skilled
senior leaders.

Scroll down and you can read all the letters of appreciation
she's had: 'Jo, I just wanted to say a big thank you for your
presentation on Friday. Colleagues are still coming up to me to
rave about your input – not bad after they have slept over the
weekend,' writes Belinda J. Jones, head of Children's Network
West. 'Dear Jo, on behalf of Coventry Secondary Heads I just
wanted to thank you very much for your inspirational session
to open our conference.' And there's no end in sight yet.

Shuter's personal website also offers the chance to see a
thoroughly professionally made film of her at work. 'This failing
inner city school was notorious for gangs and violence,' say the
words over scenes of children fighting – 'until Jo took over, in
2002. Today Ofsted describes Jo's school as outstanding. It's
in the top 4 per cent in the country' – the film having changed
to Shuter delivering an inspirational talk, then bustling about
among her pupils.

She says she leads by example, pays attention to detail and
always remembers that everyone matters. She likes to quote a line
from another head she met: 'Good school leaders have their feet
firmly on the ground but their heads in the clouds.'

The move to foundation status, paradoxically, has allowed
QK to have more genuinely comprehensive admissions criteria.
No longer forced to give priority to children from Westminster
primary schools, which sometimes meant taking pupils from the
other side of Westminster, miles away, and turning down children
from almost the next street who lived in Camden, now it takes half
its intake on a walk-to-school criterion, and the other half from
Westminster primary schools.

In December 2008, Ofsted turned up at Quintin Kynaston,
pronounced it outstanding and praised Shuter's 'inspirational'

leadership. In 2009 it was in the top 2 per cent of schools in the country for value added – the measure of how much a school improves its pupils' attainment. Nine out of ten of those in Year 11 – the GCSE year – stay on in the school's sixth form. In 2009 every one of the sixth-formers went to university and, for the first time ever, two Quinton Kynaston pupils went to Oxbridge – one to Oxford, the other to Cambridge. GCSE results have improved every year for the last ten years.

Pimlico School, despite furious parental opposition, was forced down the academy route by Westminster City Council, and in 2008 reopened as Pimlico Academy, owned and controlled by Future, a personal charity created for the purpose by John Nash, the chairman of Sovereign Capital, a private equity firm, and his wife Caroline. Sovereign Capital owns, among other things, the fee-charging schools operator Alpha Plus Group, whose schools include Davies, Laing and Dick College, an exams crammer. A new building, paid for by the government from the Building Schools for the Future budget, is going up in stages. Just before it became an academy, Ofsted visited again and pronounced it improving.

Another academy is due to appear a couple of minutes' walk from Quintin Kynaston School, just across the borough boundary in Camden. Camden Council and University College London are to build an academy so close to Quintin Kynaston that the two will inevitably fight for pupils. It will have a lot of money that Quintin Kynaston has to go out and earn, as well as a spanking new building, built at public expense, beside which Quintin Kynaston is bound to look tatty. But Shuter says: 'I have to assume that because we are a tried and tested provider in the top 2 per cent in the country, children will still come here.'

Derek Davies
The head as actor

Originally published 31 January 2008

It's called Stretford High School, but Derek Davies doesn't have any illusions about what he's really running. 'We're a secondary modern,' he says cheerfully. His local authority, Trafford, in Greater Manchester, is one of the few that still has the eleven-plus exam, and its grammar schools cream off the top 30–40 per cent of pupils each year.

He doesn't like the eleven-plus. You can't make a proper assessment at that age, and it means that each year he has to start by trying to convince his new pupils that they aren't failures. There's also an inevitability about the social profile of secondary moderns. More than a third of Stretford High School's pupils are eligible for free school meals, English is a second language for nearly half of them, three quarters are non-white, and many of the parents are unemployed.

But ironically, the eleven-plus gives Davies the most satisfying job he can imagine. 'I've no desire to work in a grammar school. There's a moral sense of purpose in teaching in a secondary modern. There isn't a day when I think "I hate this job". I love this job.' This is part of the reason why he has been able to take the school from special measures in 2004 to the top of the value-added league tables in Trafford, out-performing the grammar schools, and in the top 1 per cent nationally.

Yet teaching was not how he imagined he would earn his living when he took his Bachelor of Education at the Welsh College of Music and Drama, or even when he started his first teaching job at another Trafford secondary modern in 1987. 'I reckoned I'd teach drama for a year before going off to be a theatre director. But I found teaching compulsive.' Anyway, 'being a head is one of the biggest acting and directing jobs you can have'.

You see what he means as he walks round his school. A small, dapper, trim 43-year-old, with a clear, clipped voice, a mobile but disciplined face, a smart suit and tie and highly polished shoes, he has the air of someone who knows he's on display every moment of the day. He says a cheerful good morning to pupils he meets, and expects the courtesy of a reply. If he doesn't get it, he stops and asks for one, smiling but insistent. He marches noisily into classrooms and demands to know what's being taught, with no attempt to be discreet. He hails teachers he meets, always addressing them in a formal school manner – 'Good morning, Sir, good morning, Miss' – and they hail him back – 'Good morning, Sir'. No one seems frightened of him, but they generally do what he wants.

You can see what he means even more clearly if you log onto YouTube and search for 'Mr Davies Amarillo'. That man in the funny clothes and false nose, prancing through his school corridors and singing 'When the day is dawning on a Texas Sunday morning', is the head. It's one of this theatre director manqué's finest performances. It's not the behaviour of a head who is worried about his dignity or insecure about his authority.

And he has taken care to find solid, meaty supporting roles for every part of his school's community. The kitchen staff are there, beating pots and pans in time to the music; there's a hyperactive boy band and a girl hamming it up outrageously as sweet Marie 'who waits for me'. It's one of several interesting videos from the school which you can find on YouTube, including a rather effective anti-bullying compilation.

His assemblies are precisely targeted performances. First one of his staff had to get the lighting to his satisfaction, and he stood and instructed, a little like a leading actor who is also the director. The day I was there, Year 9 – the 13–14-year-olds – were getting their start of term pep talk. The new year, he told Year 9, is 'a chance to bury the past and start again. You know what kind of year you had in 2007. Were you a pleasure at home or were you a pain?' He drew on his drama training to do a passable imitation of a bad-tempered teenager. 'What did you do to be a good son or daughter? To make your home a pleasurable place?'

Then came the key message: 'Whatever you want, you can achieve it, if you want it that badly.' He says the same thing in different ways from the day they arrive as eleven-plus failures until they leave at sixteen (for Stretford High School has no sixth form). 'When they come here I talk to them straight away, even in Year 7, about going to university,' he tells me. 'Self-esteem, self-belief – we work very hard on this.'

It is not as difficult as it used to be to take away their feelings of rejection, he says. 'We can promote academic as well as vocational work. The curriculum is more integrated now that we no longer have different sorts of exams, with grammar schools doing O-levels and secondary moderns doing CSEs.' He remembers with pleasure a girl who wanted to be a hairdresser. 'There's nothing wrong with being a hairdresser, but when she got twelve GCSEs she said, "No, I want to go to university." Now she's doing A-levels at college and has a university place for next year.'

The school round which Davies marches, friendly smile glued to his face and clear actor's voice on permanent standby, is hardly recognisable as the one he took over in 2004. 'It was a very sad and depressing school, very little student work on the drab green walls; it just seemed shabby and not loved.' Teachers would lock themselves and their pupils into their classrooms, so as to get on with their lessons and ignore the chaos outside.

In January 2004 Ofsted placed the school in special measures. The head resigned, and Davies came in after the Easter holiday, quickly removing the solid panel with its swipe card machine which used to guard the head's office. He walked round the school a lot, saying 'Good morning' to everyone, but they all passed him with their heads down. He invited all the staff to come and see him. Some of them burst into tears in his office. He split everyone – teachers, pupils, support staff – into groups to work out what had to be done. 'This said: we're doing this together, it's not some superhead coming and saying what we're going to do,' he says. He made sure all the pupils were involved, not just the good ones. Bringing in disaffected students, Davies says, 'makes the problem part of the solution'. He remembers a group of girls of whom teachers had despaired. He describes them as 'very vocal and strong willed', which sounds like the empty political correctness of phrases such as 'challenging behaviour', but it isn't: he means it as a genuine compliment. 'By the time they reached Year 11 they were part of getting the school out of special measures,' he says.

The walls were repainted in brighter colours and are now covered with student work, some of it startlingly original. Davies spent a lot of money on computers, on creating interesting new spaces out of forgotten or unused bits of a very traditional school building, and on an attractive new cafeteria area with plasma screens showing news channels, music channels and the school's own website. Some money came from the government's Standards Fund, but he also saved money, partly by abolishing the supply teacher budget. With staff attendance at 79 per cent, this used to absorb £169,000 a year. Now staff attendance is 97 per cent. Davies raised teacher attendance partly through the unorthodox method of putting every teacher with 100 per cent attendance into an annual draw for a £50 and a £100 prize. Local papers attacked him for it, but 'I spend £150 a year and save £169,000'. He can cover the few remaining absences without supply teachers.

Naturally he did the organisational things, restructuring his management team and so on, but much more was probably achieved by changing the environment, and by the spring in his step, the bounce of his personality and his evident love for the children in his care (he has none of his own). 'You have to like children to do this,' Davies says. 'You can tell the teacher who likes children.' Every child in the school gets a birthday card every year, personally signed by the head.

Four years after it had placed Stretford High School in special measures, Ofsted was describing it as 'outstanding', and in 2007

Davies began a second revolution. 'At first, I emptied the corridors, rebuilt confidence in teachers. Now we can move to the next stage.' He abandoned the traditional school day. Since 2007 there has been no mid-morning break from 10.45 to 11.00, and no bells ring every forty minutes or so. Teachers take a break when they think they should, and the bright new canteen, where there will soon be a cyber café and a smoothie bar, is busy all the time, from 7.45 a.m. to 5 p.m. So on Wednesdays, Davies teaches English (he thinks it's important for the head to visit the chalkface every week) for a solid four hours, taking breaks when he thinks he or the class need them. 'Some will take advantage but the minority should not be allowed to dictate what you do.'

His friendly confidence seems to infect the school. A boy of fifteen approached me to say that he wanted to be a journalist, and asked detailed and intelligent questions about the best way to go about it. Teachers, pupils, cleaners all smiled at me and said 'Good morning' even though Davies wasn't there to make them. Every actor knows that you start with the externals – the smile, the false nose. The rest will follow.

Update

A month after I visited, in February 2008, Ofsted pronounced the school 'outstanding'. 'We'd gone from special measures to outstanding in four years,' said Derek Davies with pardonable pride. Results that year were remarkable: half the pupils got five A*–Cs at GCSE including English and maths. That's higher than the national average – in a secondary modern school.

The change of the school day was one factor. It worked a treat, he told the *Times Educational Supplement*. 'If you want a learning culture, then every decision you make has to be based around it. So, for example, we don't have timetabled breaks at school – we have a break when there's a dip in the learning, and have wraparound service from breakfast to tea. Everyone at Stretford is a learner.'

Davies left Stretford High School in 2009 to become principal of the new Droylsden Academy, and he will take his ideas further there. A new building will open in 2011 and it will be built around his educational principles. 'It's a very different sort of design which puts learning skills at the forefront,' he says. It will consist of a hub and four spokes round it, with different spaces where pupils can go to learn and research, and far fewer traditional classrooms than you would expect.

The chance to start a new school and design a new building was in the end irresistible, but the move was 'the hardest decision I've ever had to take' because 'my heart is in that school. Sometimes I still think: why did I leave?' And in some ways he feels he is going back to what he had to do in his first days at Stretford. Droylsden Academy is formed from two schools which have been closed, a boys' school which was failing and a girls' school which he describes as 'coasting'. So it's back to walking the corridors and insistently saying 'Good morning' to everyone.

Stretford, meanwhile, shows no sign of regressing without him. Its new head is his old deputy, Eddie Malone, by all accounts a very different sort of character: not a showman at all, but careful and methodical. Perhaps just the right man to consolidate what Davies achieved.

William Cotterell
The head as farmer

Originally published 6 March 2008

According to Ofsted, Homewood School, near Tenterden in Kent, is 'a comprehensive school . . . in a local authority also providing selective education'. This is illiterate rubbish, like saying that all schools in Kent are equal but some are more equal than others. You can't have a comprehensive school in a local authority also providing selective education, because a comprehensive school by definition gets children from all ability ranges.

But Homewood, whose 2,100 pupils and scattered collection of buildings of various styles and periods give it the feel of a university campus rather than a school, gets close to squaring this circle, with pupils who positively choose it over the local grammar schools, and (it has to be said) an intake which, as we will see, ensures it gets a few bright, motivated children.

Polly, who showed me round, is a Year 10 pupil who refused to sit the eleven-plus because she might then have had to go to the girls' grammar school, and she wanted to come to Homewood. And if Polly – bright, confident, clever, thoughtful – couldn't have walked into the grammar school if she'd wanted to, then the eleven-plus is an even bigger ass than I took it for.

'The selective process is a dreadful piece of social engineering,' says Homewood's cheerful, exuberant, bearded and amply proportioned 53-year-old principal, William Cotterell. 'I don't understand why, in the twenty-first century, we tolerate this outdated system.' Back in 1997 he had high hopes that the new Labour government would change it,

and he is uncharacteristically unforgiving about its failure to
do so.

As a foundation school, Homewood can set its own admissions
criteria. First it takes pupils from all the local villages. Those
outside the catchment area can sit a test, and the top 20 per cent
also get into Homewood. It's not a compromise Cotterell likes,
and the inevitable result, he says, is: 'You get kids in Ashford
getting on buses to come here, and kids next door to the school
getting on buses to go to grammar school in Ashford.' But, he
says: 'This gives us a balanced intake and helps us to maintain our
comprehensive nature.' It's the reason why, however implausibly,
he disowns the term 'secondary modern'. Homewood has a very
mixed intake – not overwhelmingly poor, as many secondary
moderns are, but with some very poor pupils – and, oddly if
you are used to city schools, overwhelmingly white.

But Cotterell lives in the world as it is, not as he thinks it ought
to be. He's proud of doing better in value-added league tables
than the grammar schools. According to Ofsted, his 'vigorously
articulated confidence . . . infuses the whole school with a shared
vision and buoyancy'. At sixteen and at eighteen, pupils' average
standards are around the national average, which, as Ofsted puts
it, 'represents good progress for most students'.

On some measures the school does remarkably well, given that
the grammar schools cream off many academically able children.
Some 68 per cent of its pupils get five A*–Cs at GCSE, compared
with a Kent average of 65 per cent and a national average of 61
per cent. Its A-level score of 556.5 is of course dwarfed by those of
Kent's grammar schools, but would not disgrace a comprehensive
school in a non-selective area – though there are some other Kent
secondary moderns which do marginally better. In value-added
league tables it does better than the county's grammar schools.

Many local pupils and parents make a positive choice to go to
Homewood rather than to a grammar school, as Polly did. 'Parents
are far more aware now of what schools are about,' says Cotterell.
'What they see when they come here is a range of facilities, resources
and courses.' He thinks his own daughter, now eight, is likely to

choose Homewood, and he will encourage that. 'She's grown up with this school and sees it for what it is, a range of opportunities.'

If he could rerun his own schooldays, Cotterell would never have gone to his London boys' grammar school. He doesn't approve of single-sex schools, and the grammar school made him choose between his two greatest interests, music and science. It did not have the wide variety of choices that he is so proud of at Homewood. 'The expectations were all to do with the most able,' he says. 'I didn't want to be a lawyer or a doctor, or go to Oxbridge. I knew I wanted to be a teacher.'

So he went to Keele University in 1973 to study education and geography, then taught in Staffordshire, partly in the mining community of Rugeley. 'You looked across the playground and all you could see was the pithead and cooling tower, and you wondered what their aspirations could be.' It was there that he saw what education can do: 'You could see hope and expectation on the faces of the pupils.'

In 1992 Cotterell went to Homewood as director of the sixth form and of community education, moving up to become vice principal to Derek Adam. The two of them set about a series of innovations which have helped make Homewood an over-subscribed school, despite Kent's selective policy. 'Between us, we brought the school to where it is now,' he says. When Adam retired last year, Cotterell became principal. By then, much of the running of the school had already been delegated to him.

Adam and Cotterell changed a great deal, but one thing they never considered changing was the school farm. It's a proper working farm, it sells eggs and lamb, and his farm manager, Andrew Town, proudly displays certificates for the many prizes they win all over the county. But it is also used for teaching in science, geography, English and maths. 'A head here could get away with changing anything except that. It's been here for a very long time, and is an integral and greatly valued part of the school. It says: a school is about learning for life,' says Cotterell.

The school has a young farmers' club which anyone can join. Homewood's young farmers are a dedicated bunch. 'If you

allocate a student to feed the calves, they must have commitment
– calves need feeding at weekends as well,' says the enthusiastic
but inappropriately named Town. 'They have to work hard to
achieve those prizes.' The farm offers open days for the local
community, and its animals include calves, reared from ten days
old, sheep, pigs, goats, rabbits, guinea pigs, chickens, ducks and
geese. Cotterell plans to use the farm produce on catering courses,
once he can overcome the health and safety obstacles.

The farm was sacrosanct, but Cotterell and Adam changed
a great many other things. The school year comprises five terms
of eight weeks each. In the first two years pupils take a 'total
curriculum' in which all the main subjects go into a thematic
course. So, for example, the history teachers have developed a
thematic way of looking at the Norman Conquest, with inputs
from other subject teachers. Cotterell explains: 'How do you get
an army from northern France to England? What's it going to be
like for a Norman soldier coming here? How do you report that
to someone else? Once the Normans have come here, they are
immigrants – what's that like?'

He is trying to escape from the tyranny of taking exams at set
ages, and pupils can sit public examinations early if they are ready
for them. Homewood makes everything as flexible as possible,
ensuring that pupils do not have to choose between academic and
vocational courses. 'If a child wants to look at applied learning,
why not? I have kids who are doing painting and decorating
alongside an A-level course,' he says. He likes to devise the
curriculum, as far as possible, round each individual child. 'We
look at the profile of each child when they come into the school,
and ask: what is the best curriculum model for that child to lock
into?' The students I spoke to felt enthusiastic about the wide
range of choices.

The school has what Cotterell calls vertical tutor groups.
Instead of a tutor group consisting of pupils from the same year,
it will have pupils all the way from Year 7 to Year 10 – pupils
from age eleven to age fourteen rubbing shoulders with each other
and learning from each other, which he says gives almost 'a sense

of family'. The management system, meanwhile, is as devolved as it can be, so that the huge school is almost a collection of mini-schools of 300 or so pupils each, and he has a management team of no fewer than seventeen.

Not that any of this frenzied change stops Cotterell from having fun. Until a few months ago he was the lead singer in a staff band which was good enough to get commissions for gigs locally. Now, however, one band member has retired, and two have gone to other schools.

Unusually for the head of so big a school, Cotterell finds it important to visit the chalkface every week, and his style of teaching is rather like his style of management: cheerful, friendly, relaxed and theatrical. I watched him bring alive, with liberal use of hand gestures and colourful imagery, a rather dry survey of criminal law for sixth-formers. At one point, the class burst out laughing as something reminded them of a case he had described last time, when someone sued after a microwave exploded in his face.

Then he brought me in. Our journalist visitor, he said, wanted to find a suitably humiliating photograph of him. What had I come up with, he wanted to know? I said I wanted him to go the farm and be photographed with the animals. 'See what I have to put up with?' said Cotterell. 'Ritual humiliation, that's what it is.' The sixth-formers laughed, and the principal tramped off good-naturedly to feed the calves and inspect the chickens for the benefit of my photographer.

Update

Since I looked in, Homewood has spent a lot of time working with other local schools, and has come up with something rather remarkable: an arrangement that, Cotterell believes, will make it unnecessary ever to exclude a pupil permanently.

Permanent exclusions are the great failure of the education system. Most of us sympathise with a school which insists it can no longer accommodate the pupil who is so disruptive that no learning can take place when he or she is present, or is a danger to other children and teachers. Few of us would blame a school that permanently excluded a child who brandished a knife. But excluded children grow up to be illiterate and innumerate adults on the fringes of society, because they are untaught; and Britain's prisons are full of those who cannot read and write, because increasingly there is no way for them to make a living except by crime – often violent crime. Half of Britain's prisoners have a reading age below eleven, according to Home Office figures.

So schools in the Ashford area have reached an agreement not to exclude permanently, but to give those children who are causing the greatest problems a tryout in another school – or as Cotterell puts it, 'managing the marginal pupils between the schools'. Shifting them around the schools has worked, he says. 'So far we have been able to hold the line. We move a child and then rebuild their engagement with learning.' It's one aspect of a growing involvement with other local schools, as part of which Homewood will open a primary school in 2012. It is also part of a growing community involvement, which sees the school engage itself heavily in adult education.

But Cotterell understands that the sort of co-operation between schools that he seeks is made harder by Kent's selective policy, which sees some children going to the grammar schools and others to the secondary moderns. 'Grammar schools are not about learning but about social preference and division,' he says.

There are interesting things happening at Homewood – but Cotterell is not staying around to see them. He's taking very early retirement, aged only fifty-four, and a new head teacher will take over in 2010. Cotterell is off to do something right outside education. What is it? He's not telling.

Sue Seifert
The head as anti-fashion statement

Originally published 10 April 2008

Short of putting on crushed velvet trousers and saying 'Peace, man' it's hard to see how Sue Seifert could be less fashionable. All the time I was with the head teacher of Montem Primary School, in the London Borough of Islington, she didn't once say 'drive standards up' or 'restructure my management team' or even 'deliver quality education'.

Her outfit could not have been less like power dressing if she had avoided it deliberately, but I am sure she hadn't. If she thought anything it was 'I must have a clean pair of trousers somewhere'. The trousers were complemented by a stray shirt tail that had escaped the tucking-in operation. Her staff follow her lead. This is not a suit and tie school.

She's sixty-two, quite short, with errant grey hair, and due to retire next year. She left the Communist Party when it split in 1991, but her radical politics haven't changed – if anything, forty years as a teacher have reinforced them, she says.

Andrew Adonis [schools minister at the time] knows nothing about the real world and is poison to education. When I started teaching we knew of children who couldn't come to school because they had no shoes. That stopped – and now it's started again. How dare politicians talk of benefit cheats when you see them cheating on their expenses!

A sign above her desk reads: 'It will be a great day when

our schools get all the money they need, and the air force has to hold a cake sale to buy a bomber.' She's an unreconstructed believer in letting children play, and thinks the government's rigorous testing regime and obsession with league tables steals their childhood.

If she didn't get good results, she would be damned as a 1960s relic, and replaced by a suit with an MBA. As it is, the suits come to her for advice. After several successful years running another Islington school, the council made her a troubleshooting head and sent her to sort out schools in trouble.

That was her mission when she arrived at Montem in 1998. The school serves one of the most deprived areas of north London. Three quarters of its 450 children have English as a second language, and two thirds are eligible for free school meals. The junior and infant schools had just merged, and the merger had gone wrong. Teachers were leaving in droves, SAT results were dreadful and the council was talking of closing the school. Ofsted wanted to place it in special measures, but agreed to talk only of 'serious weaknesses' if Seifert was prepared to stay for two years. 'The children didn't feel safe because the adults weren't in control,' she told me. 'And when children feel unsafe they get out of control. We had some good teachers, but they went into their classrooms and shut the doors so they could get on with it.' The building was 'a dump' with peeling walls, no playground equipment and no toys for the younger children.

But 'a school can always be saved. If it's failing it's always because of poor management and leadership.' She made children feel safe again, gave teachers their own budgets to spend on materials, and stopped parents from barging into classrooms and shouting at teachers. They had to come and shout at her instead. The first mother who did so stood in her office and screamed. Seifert said: 'I'm sorry, I can't hear you.' The mother shrieked louder, and Seifert continued to claim she could not hear. The mother burst into tears, and later went to the playground and told other parents: 'If you shout she can't hear you.'

Ofsted came back two years later and pronounced it a good school. Seifert cares not a jot for SAT results – 'Everything has to be measured, and have targets, and layers and layers of management' – but her school's SATs results are in the mid-range for Islington, which is good since it serves some of the borough's most deprived estates. Children are taught French from the age of eight.

She doesn't structure her day. She deals with things as they walk through her ever-open door, and since her office is right by the school entrance, most things do walk through it. Teachers, parents, children, cleaners, secretaries wander in more or less at will and start a conversation with the head, and she gives them all her full attention and as much time as it takes.

She starts the day with an amble round the playground, collecting children's mobile phones, which they will get back before they go home. Back in her office, a supply teacher arrives and wanders naturally through the head's door. Seifert says: 'We want you to do Year 2 today. They're a tough class and you're really good at behaviour management.' Next comes a mother distressed that her ten-year-old has not got the secondary school place she wanted. Seifert sympathises, advises, makes a phone call to find out how far down the waiting list the child is, explains appeals procedures, and offers to help draft an appeal. Then there's a boy who's been sent to her for fighting. He's not a bit frightened, and he doesn't get shouted at, but he's upset because he's displeased her. Teachers wander in and out, collecting things from Seifert's cupboard or placing in her locked drawer mobiles that have somehow missed the morning's trawl.

Then there's a man from the council. Seifert managed to get her hands on a building by the school, and she is doing it up with £50,000 she got from some nearby developers, which was the council's price for letting them build on a neighbouring site. The man is here to check on the work. She tells him what it's going to be – a community house, a family learning centre, a breakfast club. Has she written terms and conditions for those who use it? No: 'Businesspeople do that.' But she ought to have them, he says. 'I'll talk to my chair of governors, she's a businesswoman.' But Seifert isn't as scatty as she likes to appear. He knows he'll get his paperwork. He says: 'Family learning and community education is your legacy here – it ought to be called Sue Seifert House.' She says, no, it's going to be called The Community House.

The Seiferts are a well-known radical north London Jewish family. They were not religious, but strongly culturally Jewish – 'We did Passover.' Her father, Sigmund Seifert, born as his family fled from the Polish pogroms, founded the left-wing law firm Seifert Sedley, joined the Communist Party, and was the libel lawyer for the communist paper the *Daily Worker*. Sue, her sister and two brothers – one is the well-known left-wing lawyer Michael Seifert – had 'a wonderful childhood' in Highgate, where their large house accommodated Communist meetings and played host to some of the famous radical figures of the time – she remembers particularly Vanessa Redgrave and Alfie Bass.

Her father told his daughters: 'It's a man's world, so whatever you do, you have to do it three times as well as a man.' Both went to Camden School for Girls, whose head, Doris Burchill, she credits for turning her into a teacher, as well as for letting her think for herself. 'We had school elections, I stood as a Communist, and she gave me a platform!' But they did fire her as house monitor for wearing a CND badge.

She trained as a teacher at the Froebel Institute. The principal, Miss Brearley, thought this radical product of the 1960s was trouble. They argued about dress ('Young ladies don't wear jeans,' Miss Brearley said), about locks on the doors of their rooms (the principal thought that if they had locks, they would be promiscuous) and about pretty well everything else. Miss Brearley's reference said that Seifert was unfit to be a teacher. Fortunately, it arrived late, and the Inner London Education Authority had already given her a job.

In 1982 she became head of an Islington primary, Thornhill, which she left, after fifteen years, in much better shape than she had found it. Some of Islington's trendiest residents passed through her hands, though a few of the middle-class parents, she says, 'panicked' and sent their children to private schools. Then Islington made her a troubleshooting head.

Seifert runs a transparently happy school. Her overwhelmingly young staff seem devoted to her, and the children greet her cheerfully everywhere she goes. There's hardly an inch of wall or ceiling that isn't covered with something colourful and arresting. Attractive spaces have been carved out for younger children to play in.

Montem revels in its diversity. Madeeha and Kwame, told to show me round, took me to the map of the world in the hall, which is surrounded by a list of every child in the school under his or her country of origin. Madeeha finds her country, Bangladesh, for me, and then Kwame directs me to Ghana. The school is so far removed from the spirit of the times that I can't understand how Seifert gets away with it. Neither can she. 'I shouldn't have survived.' But she has, and I think Madeeha and Kwame will grow up to be glad of it.

Update

Sue Seifert didn't retire, and it was naive of me to believe she would. She left Montem and had about five days of retirement before Islington Council rushed her off to yet another school in trouble. 'They caught me as I was rushing out and yanked me back in,' she says, but she doesn't sound broken hearted about it. They call her executive head and let her work four days a week.

This time it was Canonbury Primary School, attended by the children of leading Islington glitterati such as London mayor Boris Johnson and former education minister Lord Adonis – ironically, since, as we have seen, she had previously described him as 'poison' to education. The head teacher, Jay Henderson, who had joined the school in 2005, was sacked after allegations that he watched pornography on a computer at the school. His judgement was already in question after he had appointed his friend Robert Stringer to teach drama. Stringer was later found to have been sacked from his previous school after a police investigation, and caused an outcry by showing his pupils the film *Shakespeare in Love*, which has several sex scenes.

Henderson had previously worked at Chaulden Junior School in Hemel Hempstead, Hertfordshire, where he was named the East of England's Head Teacher of the Year in 2004. Ofsted praised him as inspirational and said that he provided a 'firm steer'. He was suspended in October 2008 on full pay while the council carried out an investigation into allegations of unprofessional conduct. A disciplinary panel sacked him on the basis of the findings of the report, which has not been published. The governing body resigned.

The council parachuted Seifert in as executive head, to run the school while a permanent replacement is found. Now an appointment has been made, and she leaves early in 2010. 'I'll try to escape again,' she says, but admitted she would be tempted if they tried to send her off to another school in trouble.

[At Canonbury] it was all deeply unpleasant stuff and the school needed to mend; it had been badly hurt by people it trusted. Parents felt hurt because they had put their trust in the head. It will take a good two years to get it to mend properly. But the parents have stuck to the school. It's a question of rebuilding trust with people, making children feel safe. My style worked here – they needed some humour and some emotional intelligence.

Meanwhile her deputy for two years, Nick Tait, took over at Montem, and his style is rather different. 'I do tend to wear a suit and tie to work,' he confessed to me. 'There is probably a slight increase in formality. I have a slightly different leadership style – hers was very much the family approach. I am a bit more involved with evidence trails and paper – not', he adds hastily, 'that Sue ignored these things.'

They are all part of the game that heads have to play, says Tait.

'Sue had the experience to get away with not playing the game. She could afford to be more of a maverick than I can.'

'Montem will change,' says Seifert. 'Nick is a clever young man and he will bring in what he wants to do, slowly and carefully.'

David Nichols
The head as plain speaker

Originally published 28 May 2008

David Nichols's great-grandfather was a dentist, and he used
a pestle and mortar to grind the cocaine which served as
an anaesthetic. I owe this fascinating, if recondite, piece of
information to the fact that I happened to turn up at Littleover
Community School in Derby, where he is head teacher, just in time
to watch him preparing his sixth-form English class to answer
questions on Robert Browning's 'The Laboratory'.

Nichols brought with him to the classroom his great-
grandfather's pestle and mortar, and ground them together noisily
and vigorously, as the jealous poem's narrator would have ground
them when she said to the scientist: 'As thou pliest thy trade in
this devil's smithy | Where is the poison to poison her, prithee?'
Nichols said: 'It doesn't make the poison any more deadly, but it
shows the violence she's feeling.' He passed his great-grandfather's
instruments round, so that everyone could feel their weight and
solidity, and make the deep banging noise for themselves, and he
said he believes his great-grandfather also chewed the cocaine,
which was legal in those days.

Littleover has an English literature teacher for a head and is
especially proud of its drama – they still talk with excited pride
of their Christmas production of *Oliver!*. I ran across a group of
six Year 7s – eleven- and twelve-year-olds – on the grass in the
crisp spring sunshine, rewriting *A Midsummer Night's Dream* in
modern language, and they willingly acted out for me their version
of the play, in which Bottom says: 'I want to play Pyramus because

I'm a better actor than you,' and Snout comes back: 'No you're not, there's no need to show off.' A group of fourteen-year-olds were studying the dynamics of *Steptoe and Son* from a video. On one corridor wall is a Year 8 cover design for Robert Swindells's novel *Abomination*. The school is very proud of its long-serving drama teacher, Mary Bucknell, twice Derby's Teacher of the Year.

So what on earth is this hotbed of drama and literature doing as a science and mathematics specialist school? 'We only became a specialist school because the government gives you money to do that,' says Nichols, who is a plain-speaking sort. 'I don't like the idea, I think it's fundamentally wrong. Comprehensive schools should excel in all subjects. We're proud of all our subject teaching here.'

Biting the hand that feeds him is one of Nichols's hobbies. Another dollop of money was on offer if he filled in a form saying how he was going to 'transform' Littleover – 'transforming' schools being a currently fashionable bit of education management jargon. He doesn't want to transform Littleover – he's rather pleased with it as it is – but he filled the wretched form in anyway, because he always needs more money, and his first sentence was: 'There is much here that we do not wish to transform.'

And he is not going to go down the academy route. 'The government is trying to force Derby Council to have an academy by saying that if they don't, they won't get Building Schools for the Future money. But I don't want to change the status of this school.' Last December he wrote to Ed Balls inviting him to Littleover. 'I haven't even had an acknowledgement.' He thinks the visit would do the secretary of state good: 'A lot of the government approach to schools assumes that we are all failing. Education ministers need to get out more.'

You only talk like that to power from a position of strength. The school was pronounced 'outstanding' by Ofsted last year, and four of its sixth-form students have been offered Cambridge places this year. There is special help for those aiming at Oxbridge or intending to study medicine. 'I think Oxbridge still has a degree of bias towards independent schools,' Nichols says. 'There have been pupils here who I think should have been offered Oxbridge places, and were not. It is Oxbridge's loss, not theirs.'

More than nine out of ten of his sixth form go to university. And this year, when the *Financial Times* was putting together its 1,000 best schools, all the ones which were improving fastest on A-level scores were either fee-charging schools or grammar schools, except for Littleover Community School, which was in fifth place. Nichols points out that this is not a one-off blip. The scores go up steadily year by year. Last year 43 per cent of Littleover's sixth-formers achieved grade A or B at A-level; this year it is 48 per cent. At GCSE, 86 per cent got five A*–Cs. Their results often beat those of local fee-charging schools and former grammar schools.

It's easy to see why the school is over-subscribed and has a long waiting list. Yet there is no fiddling with the intake. In fifteen years as its head, Nichols has not wavered once in his determination to run 'a genuine comprehensive' with 'no selection at all, overt or covert'. Some 42 per cent of the pupils are from ethnic minorities, and 9 per cent are poor enough to be eligible for free school meals. 'We used to have 20 per cent eligible for free school meals, but as the school got better and better results, people started to buy houses nearby to get their children in, and house prices went up. You've seen that one before, haven't you?' I have. What I haven't seen before is a head who doesn't mind being quoted as saying it.

So how is it done? There is no magic bullet. There is no great structural change that has 'transformed' the school – the school day is a fairly traditional one. 'Children like coming to school, we get 97 per cent attendance, and we do a lot of pastoral work,' says Nichols. His personal style and high visibility contribute to success. 'I don't communicate by email. If I want to talk to a teacher I'll walk to the other end of the school to find them. I'm around all break and lunchtime, talking to children, getting to know them. I'm very accessible to them.' Unlike many heads, he still teaches, though only 2½ hours a week. 'I enjoy it, and I'm still good at it. It keeps me in touch.

'We don't expect staff to shout at children. Generally, if
you treat children with respect, they will respond with respect.'
Teachers are the key, he says: 'We have a lot of electronics but the
best resource is the quality of the teacher.'

High visibility enables him to set the tone of the school. You
can tell the effect when you walk round, with him or without him.
With him, you find pupils nodding and saying 'Hi, Sir' as naturally
as they might greet their friends. Without him, children and staff
alike greet you with cheerful, unabashed, confident friendliness.

Yet Nichols is not a noisy, theatrical head, with an all-pervasive
personality. With his dark suit and his low, even voice, you could
mistake him for a provincial bank manager. Born in Cambridge
in 1952, he went to a Catholic boys' grammar school, which 'put
me off religion for life'. He thinks the children he teaches at his
comprehensive get a much better quality of education than he had.
'We had no discussion about what subjects we were to do. I did
Greek instead of history because they said bright boys must do
Greek. Bullying was to some extent accepted.'

In 1970 Nichols went to Sussex University to study English –
'after Cambridge I wanted to be somewhere trendy and modern'
– deciding in his last year that he wanted to be a teacher, and
going on to do a PGCE at Nottingham University. He taught
in Loughborough, then in the mining community of Kirkby-in-
Ashfield during the miners' strike of 1984–5, then in Nottingham,
before arriving at Littleover as head in 1993.

It was just the sort of school he wanted to run. Founded in
1949 as a secondary modern, it went comprehensive in the 1970s,
which he approves of; but in 1989 the county took away its sixth
form, which he disapproved of, and he got it back in 1999. He
also brought back uniforms: 'I think children need a mindset
that says "I am at work".' Sixth-formers wear suits instead. Even
though there is a sixth-form centre in Derby, most Littleover pupils
elect to stay at school.

Nichols did not bustle in and 'transform' Littleover. The school
was already well run, he says. It had continuity: he is only the
fourth head in nearly six decades. He has not the smallest interest

in being a 'superhead', or getting overlordship of a neighbouring school, or trailing around after academy status, or in fact doing anything different at all from what he does. He just wants to go on leading Littleover Community School, because he knows, in his quiet and understated way, that he does it rather well.

Update

To David Nichols's undisguised delight, the government failed to force the two Derby schools down the academy route. He played a significant part in ensuring that failure by providing an alternative. Since 1 January 2009, Littleover and another Derby high-achiever, Chellaston Foundation School, have been mentoring two schools which had been labelled national challenge schools by the Department for Children, Schools and Families, and told to improve their results. These two, Bemrose School and Sinfin Community School, were the ones which the government had hoped to turn into academies. Littleover has taken on Bemrose, and Chellaston is responsible for Sinfin.

'The government tried to bully governors, staff and the council into making them into academies,' says Nichols. 'There was a very glitzy marketing presentation. The local authority was told it wouldn't get any Building Schools for the Future money to rebuild Derby's secondary schools unless their proposals included at least two new academies.'

Efforts to sell the academy idea included a lavishly produced booklet called *The Derby Academy* and one of those clever questionnaires which masquerade as efforts to find your opinion, but are actually designed to tell you what your opinion ought to be. 'Are there aspects of the proposed academy that you particularly support?' it asked, without giving you the opportunity to say that you didn't support the proposal at all. The 'key features of the academy' which the reader was asked to decide upon started with 'Ensuring good reading, writing and number skills' – the subliminal message being that non-academies ensured

poor reading, writing and number skills. But it all backfired,
and governors, staff, parents and pupils at Sinfin and Bemrose
fought the academy proposal to the point where the local council
and Derby College started to see that it would be politically
embarrassing to side with central government and force academies
on local people.

The local authority, says Nichols, 'was desperate for an escape
route and embraced the new idea of National Challenge Trusts,
which were much less radical and retained control of schools in
local hands. The staff, parents and governors at Bemrose are all keen
to embrace this new concept. I would not agree to anything that
was being imposed against their wishes. The National Challenge
Trust attracts £637,000 of additional government funding and is
supposed to ensure that Bemrose is in a position to achieve 30 per
cent plus [five or more A*–C GCSEs] from 2011 onwards.'

Littleover will now form a trust to take over Bemrose, with
a majority from Littleover on it. The trust will appoint a new
governing body and plan how to support Bemrose in meeting
the national challenge target of 30 per cent of pupils achieving
five A*–C grades including English and maths. Bemrose School
will have a new governing body, a new staffing structure and
possibly a new name and uniform. Littleover will provide support
and expertise in those areas where the school's need is greatest,
including the teaching of maths and the use of performance data
to set realistic targets.

But this is not the usual kind of 'transformation', the
unthinking new broom of an academy sweeping everything out
of its way. While academy sponsors always deride the previous
administration, which makes their own efforts look good, Nichols
actually talks up the state of the school before he got there.
'They have a very good head,' he says. 'Value added at Bemrose
is good and Ofsted has just rated its performance as satisfactory,
the highest it can gain with its current levels of attainment.' Any
self-respecting academy sponsor would insist that the head was a
lazy, old-fashioned nincompoop, and a dynamic hero head could
'transform' the place.

'It is very hard to raise standards with Bemrose's intake,' Nichols says. Bemrose School is an inner city school with 70 per cent of pupils from ethnic minority backgrounds. Two thirds of Year 11 pupils (15–16-year-olds) are identified as having special needs. A third qualify for free school meals. Only seven out of ten of the 2009 Year 11 cohort were at the school from the age of eleven. Attainment on entry to Bemrose is well below the national average and many of the pupils have recently arrived from eastern Europe or the Indian sub-continent.

But whatever Nichols does there, he will do it without changing the intake. 'When they wanted to turn Sinfin into an academy, they talked of not offering children from its local community an automatic place,' he says. 'That's the easy way to raise standards: get different children.'

'We will reach the 30 per cent in the short term, but it will be very hard to maintain it for the long term,' he adds, and it sounds rather shocking, for we are no longer used to this sort of honesty from high-ranking educators. Any academy sponsor would offer a travelling salesman's wide smile and say 'Failure is not an option' before picking up a clipboard and striding around looking dynamic.

As for Littleover itself, 44 per cent of pupils gained three or more A* or A grades at GCSE in 2009. After Ofsted called the school 'outstanding' in 2007 it was designated a High Performing Secondary School, which allowed Nichols to choose a second specialism, about which he cares not a jot, and to lay his hands on an extra £60,000 a year, which he cares about passionately. The money was used to upgrade the languages facilities and introduce Spanish as an additional language, making a total of five languages on offer. The school continues to enter more than nine out of ten of its students for a language GCSE, against the national trend.

Just before Christmas 2009 Nichols told the school he intended to retire in September 2010. Immediately a petition was set up on Facebook asking him to stay, which by mid-January 2010 had attracted 1,800 signatures of present and past pupils. He's delighted and touched, but immovable. 'I want to go when I'm still enjoying it and at the top of my game,' he says. He's got no plans, apart from seeing more of his elderly mother, although he might take on some sort of part-time work later on. But of one thing he's certain: 'Whatever I do, I'm not going to become an Ofsted inspector.'

Janice Howkins
The head as crisis manager

Originally published 10 July 2008

After eighteen months as a head teacher, Janice Howkins had a lot to be pleased about. Ofsted had just called Bentley Wood High School, in the London Borough of Harrow, 'a good and improving school'. The Specialist Schools and Academies Trust had given it a certificate to recognise its high value-added scores, which measure the amount of improvement pupils show while they are at the school. The next day she was to announce the second best GCSE results the school had ever achieved.

That night the school went up in flames.

She remembers exactly where she was when she heard the news. The call came through to her mobile phone at 6.30 p.m. on Wednesday 22 August 2007 in a cinema in Uxbridge, where she and her teenage son and daughter were watching John Travolta and Michelle Pfeiffer in *Hairspray*. She drove straight to the school, talking on her mobile to the schoolkeeper. (It's rather typical of this cautious, thoughtful woman, who chooses her words as though she is selecting costly jewellery, that she paused at this point in the narrative to assure me that she has a hands-free mobile, so both her hands were on the steering wheel.) The fire service wanted the home number of her head of science: they needed to ask what chemicals were stored in the laboratories. On reaching the school gate, the firefighters stopped her, but when she told them she was the head, they let her park in the street and walk into the grounds. Three of her senior staff stood and watched with her for the next five hours.

It was a grey, miserable night with a cold drizzle. Her slim frame was shivering, and one of her colleagues gave her his jacket. She thought: 'I used to run this building.' Now she could only watch flames coming out of the roof, and others dealing with it. The one decision she could take was that the following day's distribution of GCSE results was going to go ahead, even if she had to do it in the street.

That night left her with a lasting admiration for firefighters. 'They were magnificent,' she says. 'They always told us what they were doing, and why.' They did not always attack a flame with water, because they were being very careful about water damage. At 10.30, with the flames almost under control, the firefighters advised Howkins and her colleagues to go home and get some sleep, for they would be needed the next morning. She slept badly and dreamed of fire.

Driving to school the next day, she was fearful about what she might find. But the simple act of putting on her work clothes and going to school to meet pupils, parents and teachers helped her to do what she had to do. 'It placed me on the immediate route of leading the recovery programme.'

She did not know whether she was going to lose the whole school. She didn't, but the whole of the upper floor was destroyed. The next morning, with the flames extinguished, the firefighters encouraged her to go inside, though she did not want to. 'It felt like an unknown building. It was totally dark and full of water. I felt very sad. But I knew that the lockers were empty, so none of the girls had lost their work.'

It's still not clear what caused the fire – it may have been an electrical fault. Arson is not suspected.

There were some temporary mobile classrooms beside the building, which were undamaged, so they were used the next day to give out the GCSE results of which Howkins was so proud: more than two thirds, 67.4 per cent, had achieved five A*–Cs at GCSE – and including English and maths, the figure was still 61 per cent. They were the second highest results in a decade, a shred below the previous year's 69.5 per cent.

This is not a selective school, nor is it in an affluent area. A quarter of its very ethnically mixed 700 girls are poor enough to qualify for free school meals. But it is over-subscribed and has to keep a waiting list of pupils who want to come in. There are a few big, expensive houses nearby, but the children from those homes mostly go to fee-charging schools – though Howkins is transparently sincere in her conviction that there is nothing an expensive school can give them that Bentley Wood can't offer.

She does not claim to have 'transformed' the school, a claim that seems to be de rigueur in these days of superheads. It was a good school when she took over in January 2006, and the steady improvement in its results has continued. She has developed the pupils' voice and the parental voice. She says she brings an enthusiasm for learning and for young people, and adds: 'This is the best job you can have, a very privileged job.'

Born and brought up in East Finchley, north London, Howkins loved her own schooldays at Finchley County Grammar School, and knew early on that she wanted to be a teacher. As a sixth-former, taking A-levels in English and drama, she was already helping with remedial teaching in the school. She trained as a teacher at Balls Park College in Hertford – these were the days when teachers took a three-year teaching certificate as an alternative to a degree – but later took an Open University MA in language and literacy and an advanced diploma in special educational needs, and became an English teacher.

Howkins has lived and worked in the neighbouring borough of Harrow for twenty years. For a long time, she specialised in special educational needs, but 'I became committed to young women's education and saw the value of girls' schools. Girls are often more focused on studying and have more warmth between them.' She has the figure and fluid movements of the keen athlete she is, playing netball and tennis regularly and taking skiing holidays in France.

Staff and parents have been fulsome in praise of her leadership since the fire, and I asked her what makes a good head. She is not keen on that sort of question – she is cautious about what she says, seeming to fear that an elephant trap lurks behind every phrase, and anyway perhaps what she does comes from instinct rather than philosophy. But she did explain that a good head teacher should value the people she works with – the teachers, the pupils and their families – and should empower them to lead, which is why she is keen on a pupil voice and a parent voice. And she needs to have different sorts of relationships with people in different situations.

All of which is fine – but most of the successful heads I have interviewed for this book have been natural showpeople whose noisy extrovert personalities have been an integral part of their professional personas. I told Howkins that she appears quiet, thoughtful, even a little shy. But she said: 'Every head teacher is a performer; she performs a lot of the time but in a genuine way.' As we started to walk the corridors, I started to see what she meant. She was exuding a sort of friendly, quiet authority which the girls responded to. The corridors were quiet, and she and the girls she met seemed to have a relaxed relationship. But she never drew attention to her presence. She quoted the former London schools commissioner Tim Brighouse approvingly: the head, he has said, is like the conductor of an orchestra – if she can walk away and it goes on playing, she is doing a good job. One of the ways she does that, she says, is to make everyone in the school feel valued. And right now, that includes the small army of builders the school lives with each day. She is on first-name terms with most of them, and full of praise for all of them.

The whole of the top floor, where all the maths, science and languages teaching took place, is now a building site. There was a huge hole in its roof, and, much to the head's distress, the parquet flooring was so badly damaged that it has had to be taken up and replaced with vinyl. Science and maths are currently taught in an unlovely but functional temporary prefabricated building which they call 'the village', no doubt because it is as unlike a village as anything could be.

As for the girls, Howkins's first priority from the start has been to keep them focused on learning. From that dreadful night in August 2007, her constant watchword was 'business as usual'. When the girls arrived for their results the next day, 'the grey skies and drizzle faded away, and even the pungent smell of smoke seemed to be put on hold,' she says. She was pleased that the girls were more interested in their results than in the fire. It was truly business as usual. She ran the staff training day as intended, started to teach on the planned date, and moved back into the ground floor as soon as she could. And she intends, and expects, to be giving out GCSE results this August which are at least as good as the ones she gave out that day last August.

Update

Looking back on it all in November 2009 from the comfort of her rebuilt school, what Janice Howkins is most pleased about is that the school's progress didn't miss a beat. Once again, in 2009, the school is boasting its best GCSE results ever – 74 per cent getting five A*–Cs. All its 2009 sixth-formers are going to university.

'The girls now in Year 9 chose this school despite seeing it in the state it was just after the fire. The girls in Year 10 arrived here just after the fire. We were over-subscribed when the school was a smoking ruin,' she says. Still, they were glad to be rid of the functional but unlovable 'village' and to get a new school in summer 2008, re-equipped with splendid science facilities, a new sixth-form block and resurfaced tennis and netball courts. 'The girls squealed with delight when they saw the new building,' she says. 'Something good came out of it all.'

New challenges present themselves. Harrow is one of those boroughs which used to have a middle school system and is just changing to the more usual primary and secondary school system, so this year she is welcoming eleven-year-olds for the first time. What will she do? What she's always done: focus on teaching and learning, and on business as usual. That's what she did after the fire too. 'We lost just five days, though it meant 24-hour working. And when we had our first staff training day, we spent just five minutes talking about the fire before getting on with what we were going to do anyway.'

She can do it, she says, because good teachers are far, far more important than the state of the buildings. 'I have a fantastic team of teachers. They are our most important resource.'

Jo Dibb
The head as social reformer

Originally published 12 February 2009

Once upon a time there was a north London comprehensive
school called Risinghill, where there was no uniform, corporal
punishment was banned and children had a majority on the
school council. Inspectors complained that head teacher Michael
Duane 'esteems cordiality among the major virtues'. 'Sometimes',
they said, 'in avoiding terror the school has abandoned awe.'

In 1965, after just five years, Duane was fired and Risinghill
was closed. All trace of it was expunged. The place where it
stood is now occupied by a girls' school called Elizabeth Garrett
Anderson Language College. EGA's notepaper used to say it
was 'off Penton Street' and now says 'Donegal Street' but it is
actually in Risinghill Street. It looks like – and almost certainly is –
a conscious attempt to deny the relationship with Risinghill.

So you would expect Jo Dibb, EGA's stunningly successful,
fast-talking, image-conscious head, proud of the modern-looking
logo she commissioned, insistent that everyone wears the stylishly
redesigned school uniforms and praised to the skies by Ofsted, to
play down this embarrassing connection with the 1960s liberalism
that is supposed to have taken education to hell in a handcart.

You would be wrong. She's delighted that a new study,
'Risinghill Revisited', is being prepared. When, in November, the
National Union of Teachers came to EGA to launch its study of
working-class under-achievement, Dibb drew attention to the
fact that they were in Risinghill's premises, talked about Duane's
conviction that pupils in deprived inner city schools could achieve

anything, and read out some of the things that were said about Risinghill at that time.

She says:

> Michael Duane believed in the pupils. They got rid of Michael Duane and they closed the school down, but he was a very well-regarded head teacher who then worked for the Institute of Education. In those days the school was mainly white working class, and Duane thought they could be better than anyone believed. He wanted to give them confidence, to give them all the things we want for them.

She feels the same way as Duane. Nearly half of her pupils – 47 per cent – are eligible for free school meals, which puts EGA in the most deprived 2 per cent. And she says that is an underestimate, because food shops and stalls in nearby Chapel Market lay on special deals, so many pupils do not bother to register for free school meals. Fifty-five languages are spoken, and no ethnic group accounts for more than 21 per cent of the 1,000 pupils.

Down the road is a prestigious, expensive and selective fee-charging girls' school. 'I say to parents that if you went there you would be paying £12,400 a year, and extra for this, extra for that. But you can't get a better education anywhere than you get here.' Yet children whose parents can afford fee-charging schools still stand a better chance than those from the low-income families which largely make up EGA. Poverty is inherited; you get it from your parents. Dibb has a stunning statistic to offer: of the 135,000 students with As and A*s at A-level in 2007, just 189 were poor enough to qualify for free school meals.

Breaking that link is her strongest motivation, and her results show she is making inroads. At GCSE in 2008, 56 per cent of her pupils got five A*–C grades, 44 per cent got five A*–C grades including English and maths, 95 per cent got five A*–G grades and 99 per cent got at least one qualification. That's one of the reasons why, last September, Ofsted inspectors raved about the place. 'An outstanding school in which each and every pupil really does matter,' they said. Dibb, who arrived in 2005, had improved an already good school: 'The head teacher's remarkable leadership over the last three years has ensured that the school has made further progress since its last inspection, graded as excellent, and there is outstanding capacity for further improvement.'

Yet in spite of all this, the fee-charging school girls do have an advantage, says Dibb. 'There are girls who leave EGA with a string of A*s, but if a girl from a private school and a girl from EGA walked into this room now, both equally bright, with equal qualifications, you would know straight away which was which.' The reason is 'the confidence of class'. Upper-middle-class girls know how to appeal to upper-middle-class Oxbridge admissions tutors, which is why Oxbridge still takes about half its intake from the 7 per cent of the population which goes to fee-charging schools. Dibb says:

> If you are paying that amount of money, you will make absolutely sure your daughter is there every day, that she is never sent home for any reason, that she is on time. What we have to do is to make sure we place just as much value on education as if parents were paying for it. This is just as valuable an education and in some cases better than the one you would pay for down the road.

That's one of the reasons she would like EGA to have a sixth form. As it is, the school is very close to City and Islington College, which 'we regard as our sixth form', and she has a high regard for it. Nine out of ten EGA girls go on to sixth-form education. 'If our girls get the qualifications they can have a place there, which is pretty good at that college because it is so massively over-subscribed. And we are still involved with them when they go there: we have a teacher exchange and our teachers are still involved there.'

It's also one of the reasons why Dibb felt the need, when she first arrived at the school in 2005, to 'rebrand' it. 'When I came the school had a great national and international profile but if you went down Chapel Market and said "What do you think of the school?" people would say "Terrible, shut it down".' *The Guardian* put her in touch with a design consultancy, and she sent a group of girls to work with the consultancy. That's how the new logo came about.

'The uniform was a powerful expression of who we are,' she says. 'The new uniform design gives them an element of choice. People said, "It looks like a private school." I said, "No, it's much better than that."' I offer my liberal protest about school uniforms, but she brushes it aside.

The north London middle class [she makes it clear she means me] can afford to think that uniforms limit expression. I don't want any of our girls to think they are not as good as anyone, but class is a huge issue in education.

Part of our duty in education is to give the girls a sense of occasion, of appropriate dress at a particular time. In schools like ours the sense of identifying with the school is very important. I say in assembly, 'When you go home they are all watching you, your future employers, and what do they know about EGA? The only thing they are going to know is what they have seen of you out in Chapel Market and at the bus stop. You need to think about the impression you are giving when you're out there in uniform.'

The same sort of thinking has her out in the open air market most lunchtimes, seeing her pupils relaxing and listening to the traders' opinion of them. The day I was there, a stallholder wanted to tell her that he didn't think much of a group of EGA girls he'd seen. The complaint seemed trivial to me – they were a bit spread out, apparently, and laughing, rather like teenagers anywhere – but she listened, and chatted, and promised to have a word, and he was charmed and disarmed.

A convent-educated girl from South Yorkshire, the daughter of a GP, Dibb was previously head of a school in Tower Hamlets where 55 per cent of the pupils were of Bangladeshi origin, and she welcomes the greater diversity she gets at EGA. At fifty-four she still manages an easy informality with young people. She talked to her pupils in exactly the same way as she talked to me, which made it the more disturbing when the steel suddenly came out. As we walked through the school during lesson time, three girls appeared. 'I can't believe it – not in lessons *and* wearing trainers.' They tried to slink past, but she held up a hand to detain them, and they stood, sulky but still, until she had finished.

She has the animated fluency that keeps many heads afloat, and the instinctive political skill that a London head needs. Many London heads have a habit of saying, with a self-deprecating laugh, 'I'm not a politician at all', which generally tells you that you are in the presence of a formidable operator. When I ask her what she thinks of two academies being built close by, she says: 'It's difficult to justify one school getting several times as much money as its neighbour,' then makes me read the sentence back so she can weigh it. And when I ask, in relation to the school rebuilding, whether she is suspicious that the council might sell off some of her valuable land, she says no, of course she isn't. She adds that the idea had been mentioned at one meeting and given short shrift; then that Islington planners would never allow it; and finally, that if they did, she'd chain herself to the railings. 'I know, I know, in terms of real estate, it's a wonderful location,' she agrees.

She knows exactly what she wants from the rebuilding, due to be finished by 2012, and she will get it. She wants a clear view of the new Eurostar station at St Pancras, little more than a stone's throw away. It's part of the concept of a multicultural school. 'The girls love the fact that the school is multicultural, that it is not limited by culture. The parents buy into the multicultural sense.' It's also part of expanding her students' horizons and their self-esteem, which is what she spends the best part of most days doing. 'We are looking down at the new St Pancras, this is our future, a fantastic location.' EGA pupils are not going to go on thinking they have less potential than those girls from that £12,400-a-year school, if there is anything at all Jo Dibb can do about it.

Update

The big event of 2009 was the arrival of Michelle Obama. In April that year, while her husband was meeting Gordon Brown, Mrs Obama came to Elizabeth Garrett Anderson and told the girls: 'I'm honoured to meet you, the future leaders of Great Britain.' They may not have been born rich, but they could achieve. 'There was nothing in my background that said I would be standing here today,' she said, pointing out that she was born on the wrong side of Chicago, and black as well.

EGA wasn't chosen by accident. It hit a lot of buttons for Michelle Obama: multicultural, deprived, all girls. Back in November 2008, just after Barack Obama won the US presidential election, the American embassy got in touch with the head. Would Ms Dibb like someone from the embassy to come along and talk about the struggle for civil rights in the USA? Would she like a few books for the library as a gift? Yes please, said Dibb, and someone from the embassy duly came along. 'I think they were impressed by the quality of questions and understanding,' says Dibb. They must have seen something they liked, because Dibb learned about her special visitor in February, though she wasn't allowed to tell anyone. 'I think her speech was for young girls across the country,' says Dibb.

EGA is surrounded by academies now, and Dibb's opinion of them hasn't changed. 'Whenever you have schools differentially resourced you have dislocation,' she says. But EGA is comparatively immune – 'We are secure in our reputation and the quality of what we offer.' The upward march of its results continues: in 2008, 44 per cent achieved five A*–Cs including English and maths at GCSE, but in 2009 that figure was 49 per cent. No girl left the school in 2009 without qualifications.

Joanne Dean and Sue Smith
The head as community activist

Originally published 16 April 2009

St Ives is a famously pretty Cornish town, with charming little
roads and alleyways where cars should have been banned
years ago, good restaurants, a spectacular coastal path, vast
sandy beaches and – even now – high property prices. Not, you
might think, a place where running the local school would be
challenging. Someone used to inner city schools could do it in
their sleep.

You would be wrong. Beyond the ever-expanding domain of
second homes and holiday lets, away from the sea, on top of the
hill overlooking the town centre, lie St Ives Infant School and
St Ives Junior School, two schools on one site. On the hill, too,
you will find the housing estates which accommodate most of
St Ives's permanent residents, many of whom make an insecure
seasonal living from the tourist trade (for neither of the town's old
trades – farming and fishing – employ many people any more.) The
schools take an unusually relaxed view of children going on family
holidays during the autumn term, for parents work all hours
during the summer.

About a third of the pupils have special educational needs,
and 16 per cent in the junior school and 20 per cent in the infant
school are eligible for free school meals, though that figure under-
estimates the poverty – parents in insecure and seasonal freelance
employment cannot always produce figures to back up a claim.
An inspector once said that it was like being at a school in Tower
Hamlets. The only advantages they have over inner city schools

are space, good facilities and an unrivalled view over the coast and the sea.

The head of the infant school, Joanne Dean, says: 'St Ives has a feel of wealth but the people who are servicing that are on low-paid seasonal employment. They are suffering because of high property prices caused by second-homers. Families can't afford to buy.' Dean, aged forty-five, was brought up in Salisbury and studied English at Magdalen College, Oxford, where suddenly one day she discovered that she wanted to spend her life teaching primary school children. She was helping at an Oxford community project. Taking the young children of an immigrant family to the library 'showed me that this was the most important thing there was in the world to do'.

Educating families, as well as children, remains Dean's passion. In St Ives, she says, families can be marginalised if they do not have education. More than a third of the families in the ward where the school is have no qualifications. She says: 'We are not educating children for the economy but to take control of their lives and take part in the community and be active citizens. I could see the potential of the adults here. I believe in developing people, letting them be themselves.'

So in 2003 the school began family learning. On Tuesday mornings, parents and children arrived at school together. For the first half of the morning they learned separately, with parents improving their basic skills; then parents and children would do something together. 'Parents and children enjoyed it, parents made friendships with each other and got involved with the school.' In September 2008, two outside classrooms were given over entirely to adult education, and some of the parents are now applying to university. Other parents have benefited from a family literacy class. The day I was there, Dean told the children at assembly: 'We never think to ourselves: "That's it, I have learned all I need to know." It never happens.'

She is only the third head since the school opened in 1966, and many experienced teachers have been there a long time. She lets teachers take what they want from such things as government literacy strategies and leave the rest. The government, she says, has a tendency to try to micro-manage primary school teaching. She insists that teachers need time to meet, talk and plan, and the timetable is arranged so that all teachers have an afternoon a week away from pupils.

Dean takes advantage of what the special environment can give them, marching the children down to the beach in the summer to build sandcastles and then measure them, taking them to the museum and the lifeboat station, introducing them to the local mayor and telling them they can become mayor if they want to. 'We are their first school and that is an enormous responsibility,' she says. 'If we get it wrong, other schools will have to unpick it afterwards. If you don't get their reading right, they will not get anything right.'

Hers was already a good school when she arrived in 2002 – it is now good with many outstanding features, says Ofsted. The junior school, on the other hand, was in special measures just five years ago. Sue Smith, already an experienced head teacher in the West Country, was drafted in to sort it out in September 2003: a temporary measure, but she has been there ever since.

Smith, Cornish born and bred, turned it round. Last year Ofsted called it 'a good school in which all pupils thrive' and said it had 'some outstanding features'. Pupils are 'polite, helpful and courteous and very much enjoy coming to school'. When Smith arrived in 2003, 52 per cent of the children achieved level 4 in SATs for English – it's now 77 per cent. The maths figure has gone up from 57 per cent to 77 per cent, and the science figure from 77 per cent to 96 per cent, which is well above the national average of 88 per cent.

I saw for myself that the behavioural problems Ofsted noted in 2003 are not there now. As the children came into the school assembly, Smith played quiet, soothing music. When they were all seated on the floor, she turned it off, and you could have heard a pin drop. 'What are we doing?' she asked. They knew that one. Back came the answer, from all the pupils in unison: 'We are thinking, looking, listening, not talking, and concentrating.'

As one, they folded their arms. Then the teachers came up and called out children from their class to be given special praise.

How was the change achieved? Partly, it was a matter of setting clear boundaries, Smith says, 'just like football – yellow cards, red cards'. Partly, it was improving the building. There is a new entrance and a new, light, airy library which is very high tech. She changed the colours. 'The use of blue throughout the school is a well-thought-through plan for the future linking to the sea. Blue is very calming.' Windows, doors, skylights, toilets, a 'play zone' – all have had, or are getting, structural attention.

But the key element – and, it seemed to me, the key to Smith's whole approach – was an almost evangelical faith in educational research. It's a faith, it has to be said, which is not shared by all the parents, and her occasionally jargon-laden sentences get some disparaging comments. But she is determined to find and use the latest teaching techniques, and finding time to keep up with them is a priority with her. She can quote current thinking on most topics. She says: 'I am fascinated by education research. If you went to the doctor you would not want a twenty-year-old prescription. Educational provision should be seen in the same way.'

So she cheerfully admits to being an inexhaustible source of incomprehensible acronyms. It rubs off on the pupils. Tom and Lois, the two charming and confident ten-year-olds who showed me round, told me about something called VAK, explaining that it stood for three sorts of learner: Visual, Auditory and Kinaesthetic. 'I'm a kinaesthetic learner,' said Tom. 'Engineers are kinaesthetic.' Another acronym, RAP, apparently stands for Respect, Accountability, Preparation; while on a corridor wall, huge letters spell out a third, RUCKSAC. It stands for various work tips: R for 'Read the question', U for 'Underline to understand' and so on. Moving away from the technical terms, Lois explains about Wake and Shake: just after break, the children dance to get themselves wide awake for a lesson. They show me how to borrow books from the bright and newly painted library: you put your thumb on a pad and it registers the book in your name. They tell me about the

Cornish storyteller, 'he's a friend of Miss Smith's', who comes in and does activities with them, and is fun and 'really, really Cornish'.

The walls of the head's office are covered with homespun homilies, which include 'To improve life we must improve the quality of experience' and 'Believe in yourself'. Smith's favourite is 'In times of change the learners will inherit the earth whilst the knowers will be beautifully equipped to deal with a world which no longer exists'. All right, it's a bit clumsy and clunky but you get what it means. It's an approach to education which Smith seems also to apply to her life. 'I am a vegetarian but I do eat fish with omega fatty acids in it as this will hopefully keep my memory agile and my brain really alert,' she says.

Just occasionally, correct jargon seems to take precedence over meaning. I worry a little about someone who has on their wall 'If you can imagine it, you can achieve it; if you can dream it, you can become it', because it's so obviously rubbish. The school's website begins with a vision statement: 'Learning together, free to fly', whatever that means. Then there's a mission statement which is contrastingly pedestrian, and could surely be safely adopted by any school: 'To provide high quality teaching and learning and to raise the achievement levels for all pupils.' I wish she could do without them, but it's a trivial complaint really. Smith's homilies are part of her infectious enthusiasm and drive, and it would be churlish to let them detract from her very real achievements.

Smith makes sure her staff keep up with research too, bringing leading researchers to talk to them and occasionally taking senior staff to London for conferences. The day I was there, she was videoing a maths lesson being given by one of her deputies. 'We can all watch each other's best practice. We share pedagogy,' she says. 'Ninety per cent of funding is on staff, so it pays to make sure they are good.' The staff have changed considerably since she arrived. They are younger, and she unblushingly points out that this means they are cheaper, which leaves her with more money to spend on other things. There are more men – there was just one when she came, and now she has equal numbers of men and women, which she thinks is much healthier.

Smith studied biology at Westfield College, London, took a PGCE at Exeter and started her career in 1978 teaching science in a secondary school. She has two grown-up children and two grandchildren. She says that things she loves include 'Cornwall, travel, films which make me laugh, losing myself in a good book, and anything fattening, particularly sweets and really squidgy pastries'. As with many teachers, the unhappinesses of her own childhood were part of the reason she became a teacher. She was the only one in her small village primary school to get into the grammar school, and 'I cried every day'.

She thinks there's 'a huge difference between male and female brains – we approach things differently' and she has consciously developed some male traits in order to be a good rounded head teacher. But what's her model for a good head teacher? I was expecting this research-intensive head to stump me with the name of an educational academic I had never heard of, but she confounded me by telling me it was her grandmother. 'She ran three successful farms and she was the matriarch.'

Update

Joanne Dean's determination to break the cycle of poverty by working with parents as well as children has resulted in a new programme involving the whole of St Ives: Every Child Matters. She came back from a conference inspired by similar work she had heard about in Hailsham, East Sussex, and persuaded other heads, and other local agencies, to start the programme. She says:

> There is a cycle of disadvantage in St Ives. It's a sense of history repeating itself. Families that have not been successful with their educational experience, through no fault of their own, need support if they are to help their children to a better education than they had. We want to ensure that we never have to say again 'Yes, that's what his or her parents were like'. We want to break that cycle.

So, since April 2009, schools and other agencies working with children in the town have been working together to try to break the cycle. The St Ives Every Child Matters group includes representatives from local schools, Cornwall Council and St Ives Town Council. It is collecting data on child poverty, holding meetings in the town, at which between forty and fifty people turn up, and identifying priorities for action. A grant from Cornwall Works has enabled the group to employ a project leader, and there are plans to create a community centre on one estate where a need was shown. Vulnerable children are being tracked, and a 'voice for children and young people' made up of pupils from all six schools in the St Ives area is being set up by the town council. There will be a youth council or youth panel, which, according to Cornwall Council, 'will also give children an opportunity to develop important life skills such as team working, leadership, involvement and communication as well as giving them scope to make a positive contribution to their community'.

Meanwhile Sue Smith's junior school continues to make progress – she can boast another above-average set of results in 2009. However that was achieved, it wasn't by manipulating the intake. The proportion of children eligible for free school meals has gone up to 19 per cent and those with special educational needs now account for 33 per cent, and she has had a sudden influx of new children whose families have moved into the area from the cities. In addition there are three times as many children in care as before, a worry in a county where in October 2009 children's services were condemned as 'inadequate' by Ofsted inspectors. Their report said children and young people in care were not properly safeguarded, and they identified a range of failures in care planning, risk assessment, reviews, recording, planning and visits by social workers.

But Smith is still bubbling with enthusiasm, and unrepentantly addicted to acronyms. There's a new game on the wall, identifying helpful folk like Number Nan, Alex Algebra, Data Dude and the Shape Genie.

Philip Friend
The head as succession planner

Originally published 7 May 2009

For twenty-five years Philip Friend has run a primary school which Ofsted, for the third time in a row, has just pronounced outstanding – and which is visibly a happy, purposeful place. But Friend is pushing sixty and fancies doing something else. Conventional wisdom has it that some decline is inevitable as Eccleston Mere Primary School in St Helens, Merseyside, adjusts to its first new head for a quarter of a century. The best the school can do is make the dip temporary.

Bur Friend thinks his long, careful succession planning will prove conventional wisdom wrong. In September 2008 his deputy, Yvonne Kirk, became acting head. Friend is now called executive head and spends half the week in the school. The rest of the time, he is a roving adviser to four other head teachers whose schools are in trouble.

Kirk arrived at Eccleston Mere as a newly qualified teacher in 1985. Quite quickly, Friend identified her as his eventual successor, and that early recognition, he says, is part of the secret: 'They don't identify future heads early enough. They ought to identify them when they are newly qualified teachers.' It would have been convenient for her to move on years ago – she drives 27 miles to get to work – but people seem to stay at Eccleston Mere.

What sort of school is Kirk inheriting? All those years ago, Friend set out consciously to create the opposite of the primary school he attended in a south Wales mining village, from which he remembers only playing football and being bullied. He was unhappy there and failed the eleven-plus – on purpose, apparently, and he dislikes selection at the age of eleven, saying the eleven-plus is meaningless.

He keeps a mug in his office bearing a picture of that school – a Victorian brick building blackened by coal dust – to remind himself of what Eccleston Mere must never become. So the school he runs is cheerful, noisy and colourful, like Friend himself, a small, bustling, restless, voluble Welshman. Every inch of wall is covered by children's work. As I walked round, children fearlessly attached themselves to me, to introduce themselves, shake hands and tell me what they were doing. Outside, there is a wooded play area, with logs, a shed and a beached boat, which year groups take turns to play in and which is also used for teaching. Friend developed it in summer 2007 with a £3,000 grant obtained by the parent–teacher association – the old boat and the logs were donated – and it helps to make Eccleston Mere as unlike the primary school he attended as possible.

A child who is unhappy for any reason is expected to take a pebble from a pot – there's one in every classroom – and show it to the teacher. The teacher asks no questions and makes no comment as the child leaves the classroom and goes to the small office occupied by the pastoral mentor, Diane Riley. Anything said to Riley goes no further, unless a child protection issue comes up. Sometimes she can deal with the problem easily. She keeps spare PE kits, for example. Sometimes it is something really big: bereavement, debt, divorce. Hers is an unusual role which Eccleston Mere pioneered two years ago.

Riley and Kirk are typical of the school's staff in that they have been there for a long time. Another is deputy head Sue Haslett, who started there as a newly qualified teacher twenty years ago. Over half of the teaching staff have been at the school more than a decade. It's a one-form-entry primary school with 300 children and a nursery, and if teachers like working there, they like it very much. Friend calls it a family atmosphere, and the place has a quirky familiarity all its own. Friend routinely calls teachers by their Christian names in front of the children, a practice frowned on in many schools – but even in private, teachers refer to the head as Mr Friend. I asked why, and they said it had become something like a nickname, like Mr Smiley or Mr Blobby.

Approach to discipline is informal too. In assembly, there were no teachers pursing their lips and hissing 'shh' while Kirk spoke, though the children were getting visibly restless, and I felt the teachers had let the assembly go on rather too long; yet what goes on in the classrooms seems quiet and purposeful enough.

But it's not all nurturing and family atmosphere. Friend thinks you can have all that and still do well in SATs. Last year 91 per cent of his pupils reached level 4 or better in English, 89 per cent in maths and 91 per cent in science – all well above the national average.

Several of the teachers have their own children at the school, though Friend himself had to send his daughter elsewhere until she was eight, because he does not live quite close enough to the school – they are very strict about local authority admissions criteria, and there is no special treatment for staff. Once at the school, he says, she flourished, and she is now a lawyer specialising in family and child cases. Whatever the secret of the school's success, it does not rely on manipulating its intake.

Nor does it rely on excluding the difficult ones. In twenty-five years Friend has only excluded two children, and in a very mixed area, 15 per cent of the children are eligible for free school meals, which is high but not exceptional. And although the proportion of children with special needs is not especially high, at about 16 per cent, the disabilities that children have tend to be serious ones. The school has gained a reputation for being good with conditions such as Down's syndrome, and parents with severely disabled children have been known to move house to get a place there. That's because, a few years ago, struggling to find a way of helping a seriously disabled girl, Friend came across a little-known system called Brain Solutions, which he has helped develop and used successfully in the school.

Brain Solutions begins with a detailed assessment to find which stages of a child's development were missed. For example, says Friend, if a child goes straight from lying down to walking, without going through the intermediate stage of crawling, the missed stage is likely to cause a problem later on. 'A child develops reflexes,' he says. 'If they don't, it hinders development.' Developing Brain Solutions and offering its use more widely is partly what Friend will do with the unaccustomed leisure he will have when he cuts his last ties with the school in July 2010.

The school he leaves behind is his lifetime achievement, and he is bursting with pride about it. The words he uses to describe it are 'warmth', 'happiness', 'love' and – rather strangely – 'spirituality'. Friend is not a religious man – for him the word 'spirituality' comes out of his childhood in the valleys, where God and socialism competed to make a joyful community of people who did the grim work of hewing coal from the ground.

But if you wonder how a head with these values survives in a target-centred education system, you misunderstand him. Friend has been named a national leader of education by the National College for Leadership of Schools and Children's Services and Eccleston Mere has consequently been designated a National Support School. He takes school assessment very seriously. His first advice to heads is: monitor everything that goes on, never delegate that task to someone else, and be ready with every iota of evidence when Ofsted comes to call. It matters that his attendance rates are about 95 per cent, that the school is ahead of the game when compulsory language teaching in primary schools comes in next year – they have been teaching French and Spanish for years. 'You have to play the Ofsted game. Not to do so is foolish and misguided. And every time you prepare for Ofsted, your school moves forward a bit. If you do school self-review then Ofsted is not a major problem.'

It's worked for him. In 2006 Ofsted positively drooled:

This is an outstanding school. The exceptional vision of the head teacher, which is shared with and embraced by all staff, drives forward the quality of education, so that the school is always striving to do its best for the pupils. The excellent ethos enables all pupils, whatever their talent, personal qualities or special educational need, to feel secure and to do their very best in everything.

Friend's second piece of advice to heads is: don't let the job become your whole life. Get a hobby. His is long-distance cycling, and he reckons he has cycled the equivalent of 2½ times round the world.

Friend entered teaching almost by accident. At Swansea University at the start of the 1970s, he studied natural sciences and surveying, and when he took his degree, decided at the eleventh hour to spend a year studying for a PGCE. Eccleston Mere has been almost his whole career, and he became its head at the remarkably early age of thirty-two, even then still thinking he would leave teaching one day and go out and change the world. But 'it got under my skin and I never wanted to leave it. It became so important to me, and it's been my life. When I had been there twenty years I realised I couldn't just walk away one day.'

He will be around to help and guide his successor until summer 2010. It works because he identified his successor early and Friend and Kirk are close. He developed a winning formula, and she sees no reason to change it.

Update

By the end of 2009, Philip Friend was down to two days a week at Eccleston Mere and was spending the other three days helping other St Helens primary schools, which are, in the euphemistic language of educational jargon, 'in challenging circumstances'. He has seen one of them out of special measures and guided two more through an Ofsted inspection.

He will be sixty in March 2010, and the original plan had him leaving Eccleston Mere for good in the summer, but he might stay on for another year, even though Yvonne Kirk is now fully in control. Whatever happens, 'I'll never leave the school spiritually'.

He's set out his blueprint for running a successful school on his website. Here's his formula:

› Make your school a memorable experience for children and adults, something they will remember all their lives.
› Let yourself fall in love with the place and the people and let them fall in love with you. You will get so much from them.
› Say a few words to all adults each day. It is a minute to you but it will mean everything to them.
› Take on people that are more intelligent and talented than you are. Don't be afraid of their strength or their intellect . . . you need them.
› Treat staff like balloons. Hold the strings but let them fly . . . they will innovate, initiate, develop, organise and so much more.

He is now a consultant, advising other heads, and a national leader of education for the National College for Leadership of Schools and Children's Services. Here are some of the things he tells heads:

'You don't have to be nasty to be strong.'

'You can't run it if you're not in it. Many head teachers' meetings, courses and seminars are a complete waste of time. Stay in your school with your children and adults.'

'Talk to children all the time. Don't shut your door often. Always wander around.'

'Monitor, monitor, monitor! You need to know exactly what's going on. Don't easily pass this responsibility to others.'

'There are only two sorts of organisations, those going forwards and those going backwards. Constantly self-evaluate and self-reflect to ensure forward momentum.'

'Include . . . it really can work.'

'You really do need governors. Cultivate strong relationships.'

'Get a hobby. Keep your body moving. Try to stay fit.'

'It's not very British, but strive to be the very best! Not the best you can, but the very best!'

And he is still marketing Brain Solutions.

Back at the ranch, Kirk really does not mind having her

predecessor hanging about the place two days a week. She likes it, in fact. She understands that some other people might find it irksome. 'Our situation is unique because we've worked together for so long. There's twenty-five years of experience there and I'd be foolish not to make use of it.'

They have stayed ahead of the foreign languages game. As all primary schools are being told to start teaching foreign languages, Eccleston Mere is expanding them. It now teaches French in Year 3 – to eight-year-olds – then German in Year 4, Spanish in Year 5 and French again in Year 6. Don't the children forget all their French when they have two years away from it? 'The important thing is to give them an awareness of language, it matters less which language it is,' says Kirk. The school's own teachers are learning to be language teachers.

But what really pleases her, she says, is that the school hasn't missed a beat because of the change in leadership. I spoke to Kirk again in November 2009, just as the value-added results arrived on her desk, and they showed that the school's children had done substantially better than had been predicted. The long, careful succession planning worked just the way it was supposed to.

Liz Quinn
The head as manager

When Liz Quinn took over as head at what is now called
Stourport High School and Sixth Form Centre, in Stourport-on-
Severn, Worcestershire, in 2000, 'I had a clear idea that we had
to be the architects of our own fate or someone else would do
it for us'. She set out to be the architect. It was not all pleasant
or kind, but she has made sure that no one else chooses the
school's future.

The area had middle schools, but it was changing to fall in
line with most of the rest of the country, so that those schools
would disappear and the high school would have to start taking
children at the age of eleven, which meant preparing for an extra
750 pupils in 2007. The school served one of the twenty most
deprived wards in the country, including a travellers' site, which
presented one set of problems; it also served a relatively wealthy
community which could afford to flee to the fee-charging schools
in nearby Worcester if the parents were not satisfied with what
Quinn had to offer. Other local state schools were perceived,
rightly or wrongly, as offering a better education than Stourport,
which was under-subscribed. The school, though not failing, was
certainly struggling, and in 2000 the new head was sure it needed
a new direction.

'We have a significant number of parents who do not have a
good experience of the education system,' she says. And she knows
what that means. She has seen bad experiences of education first
hand. After graduating in education and geography from Leeds
University in 1981, she took her first teaching job in Armley,
a deprived part of Leeds right next to the prison, and found

a seven-form-entry school, but only two of the forms
were expected to take any exams. So five sevenths of the
school could not read or write very well. The poverty was
unbelievable, the commitment to education was transitory, and
the majority didn't see any point to their education as they
were not to take exams.

Expectations of children and teachers were so low that
Quinn was judged a success just because she could keep the
children in their seats. The school was doing the best it could
in poor circumstances.

She thinks it would be hard to find a school like that now.
'Since then I think we've woken up to the fact that we have to
invest in education,' she says. It was a harsh start to a teaching
career, and from it 'I learned to be firm and clear, and not to move
about basic principles'.

From Armley Quinn moved to Sowerby Bridge, near Halifax,
and then to a big comprehensive school in the Midlands before
arriving in Stourport as assistant head, becoming head in 2000
and setting about making the changes she thought necessary.
Some of these were difficult, painful and controversial, and Quinn
will never earn a National Union of Teachers accolade for best
employer. But she did earn the local reputation of having 'an iron
fist in a velvet glove', which she rather glories in – she told me
about it before I read it anywhere or heard it from anyone else.

She puts the problem with which she felt she was faced like
this: 'There were some nice people working here who were not
doing the job that needed to be done. It was not easy – members
of the governing body were their friends. But several people had to
go.' The process of changing from a middle school system provided
the opportunity. Everyone in the schools had to apply for their
own jobs, and no one was safe. 'We were only prepared to appoint
those who understood what we wanted to do. It was not always
easy nor always happy,' Quinn says, in a voice which has so much
of the iron fist in it that I found it hard to perceive the velvet glove,
though I will take her word for it that it's there somewhere. 'I had

to carry out 500 interviews to make sure 180 staff were appointed in time; we had nearly 50 per cent of new teachers and 750 new pupils, a critical mass. It was the biggest challenge I and my colleagues had ever faced.'

Other initiatives were pleasanter and less controversial. She made it one of her first duties to visit the travellers' site.

> I had tea with the mums. They needed to trust me and it helped to know that I came to their ground. A lot of our staff do that now. Most parents want the best for their children and the travellers are no different in that. They had to be convinced that the school is a safe and happy place for their children to be in. The key questions for a head teacher to answer are: What's the atmosphere like? What are the quick wins to get people believing in you? The reaction they get when they say what school they go to matters to the lives of the children.

The relationship with the travellers went further than that – she employed a former traveller, Kathleen Jones, to work in the school. 'That says: we think the travelling community has something to offer us,' Quinn explains. Jones, whom Quinn taught when she was fourteen, is now twenty-one and training to be a teaching assistant, and in 2007 she arranged for the staff to visit the travellers' site in groups.

She adopted a Latin motto. Quite what message that gave out I am not sure, but she found it in the school archive and it was adopted a year after she became head. It's *Carpe Diem* – Seize the Day. And she had a new uniform designed after consultation with students, many of whom apparently thought only 'proper' schools – they meant fee-charging schools – had smart uniforms with blazers; schools like theirs had to make do with sweatshirts. That was it: smart uniforms with blazers were ordered, and the wearing of them is strictly enforced. 'A uniform does not make you cleverer or work harder,' Quinn says. 'But it is a useful way for students to identify themselves as part of our community.'

And she changed the curriculum to reduce the emphasis on traditional school subjects and bring in more vocational subjects. That seems to run counter to the rest – the Latin tag, the blazers – but she says: 'We are the town school. We need to be flexible enough to deal with all sorts of different learners. Many of our students are kinaesthetic learners.'

The ruthlessness she applies to staff is evident in what she says about the behaviour of pupils too. Staff are told, on bad behaviour by pupils, 'tackle it, don't tolerate it', and on learning, 'get them in, get them learning, get on with them, get them out'.

The Stourport High School and Sixth Form Centre opened its doors in September 2007 as an 11–18 mixed comprehensive school with 1,450 students, replacing the former 13–18 Stourport High School. By then it was clear that something had worked for Quinn. In January 2009 Ofsted described the school as outstanding – the head burst into tears when she heard, apparently. Ofsted inspectors said it had faced 'many challenges when it started over a year ago on the former high school site, including building work and temporary classrooms to accommodate the new year groups'. They added that the school 'deservedly has an excellent reputation in the local community. Parents are overwhelmingly supportive of the school and comment very positively on the dedicated staff, and the excellent care and support provided for all students.'

The school has specialist status as a language college, a training school and a sports college. Being a training school means that most of its teachers are trained as 'mentors' – guiding, supporting and assessing trainee teachers. There are now 200 in the sixth form; two thirds of the pupils go into the sixth form, and many of the rest continue their education at the local further education college. August 2009 saw the school's best-ever GCSE results: 74 per cent of students achieved five or more GCSE grades at A* to C compared to 63 per cent in 2008, which in itself was the previous best performance. The number of students achieving both English and maths also rose by 7 per cent in 2009. If you include English and maths, 46 per cent achieved A*–C grades. In 2009 Quinn won the Royal Air Force Award for Head Teacher of the Year in a Secondary School.

And now she looks as though she's going to have a new building. It will be built on a Private Finance Initiative contract and is to go up directly behind the current building. When the new building goes up, the old one will come down, and she is involved with every detail of the design.

Paul Patrick
The head as anti-racist

Cardinal Wiseman School in Ealing, west London, is proud of its head teacher. Its website trumpets a 'track record of outstanding achievement', starting in September 1997, when 'a new Head teacher, Mr Patrick, arrives'. In 1998 and 1999 the school's GCSE results were the best it had ever known. In 1999 it was named the second most improved school in London by the *Times Educational Supplement* and one of the country's best technology schools by the Technology Colleges Trust. The next year Ofsted called it 'outstanding'. And so on, for pages after page, right up to another 'outstanding' from Ofsted in 2008 and one from the Roman Catholic diocese of Westminster in 2009.

What the website doesn't tell you is that Paul Patrick hasn't been allowed into the school since March 2009. He is suspended on full pay and barred from entering the school or speaking to anyone associated with it, and no one wants to talk about him, least of all the diocese of Westminster, which once lionised him but now seems embarrassed at the mention of his name.

And yet, if any one person did take this dreadful, failing school, where no child was safe, no teacher got any job satisfaction, no parent wanted to send their children and only about a third passed their GCSEs, and turned it into a happy, safe, purposeful place with good results which local people compete to get their children into, it was Patrick.

In Ealing, this Catholic comprehensive was known as a rough, under-achieving school. Catholic families avoided it if they could. One member of staff was widely quoted as calling it 'a battleground'. The year before Patrick arrived, a pupil was stabbed just outside the school gates and died in a teacher's arms.

Six years later, in 2003, the *Times Educational Supplement* and the Catholic newspaper *The Tablet* ran admiring profiles of this by now highly successful head and his model school. The school's website still, as I write in January 2010, carries his name on its home page, and it charts his triumphant progress, without mentioning that he is no longer in charge, under the headline 'Track record of outstanding achievement'. Some of it is worth reproducing:

September 1997	A new Head teacher, Mr Patrick, arrives.
August 1998	Year 11 GCSE examination results set new record pass rate for the school.
August 1999	Year 11 GCSE examination results beat 1998 results and set another new record pass rate for the school.
November 1999	School named as second most improved state school in London 1996–9 (*Times Educational Supplement*, 29 November 1999).
April 2000	School receives an 'Outstanding' Ofsted inspection report.
June 2000	School named as one of Top 50 schools in the country (*Daily Express*, 14 June 2000).
August 2000	A hat-trick, 1998, 1999, 2000! Year 11 GCSE examination results set another new record pass rate for the school.
November 2000	School named as: Fourth most improved school in the country; No. 1 most improved mixed comprehensive school in the country; No. 1 most improved Catholic school in the country (Department for Education and Employment).

January 2001	School receives Gold Star award, from chief inspector of Ofsted, for outstanding progress.
August 2001	Year 11, predicted to get only 19% 5+ A*–C at GCSE (Year 7 entry tests), achieve 60%.
August 2002	Year 11 GCSE examination results set a new record pass rate for the school . . . 76% of students achieve 5+ A*–C!!
June 2003	Best ever KS3 SATS results . . . English 92%, maths 80%, science 80%.
August 2003	Year 11 GCSE examination results . . . a fantastic 93% of students achieve 5+ A*–C!!
January 2004	School named in 20 top comprehensives (*The Times*, 15 January 2004). School named in Top 40 value added 14–16 results (*The Times*, 15 January 2004).
August 2004	Year 11 GCSE results in the 90s again and best ever A-level results.
August 2005	New SATS record!! New GCSE record!!! 96% of students achieve five or more A*–C grades. New A-level record!!
April 2006	Ofsted inspection result: 'Outstanding'.
August 2007	Year 11 achieve 97% A*–C, which places the school in the Top 20 comprehensive schools in the country.
December 2008	Ofsted inspection rates the school 'Outstanding', including an 'Outstanding' grade for the sixth form.

And the website history ends with this inspiring rallying cry: 'There is more to come! We keep our promises!'

All these achievements turned to ashes in Patrick's hands in March 2009.

Paul Patrick was born in West Belfast in 1955, the son of a Catholic mother and Protestant father. His grandfather was the master of an Orange lodge and refused to go to his son's wedding because he was marrying a Catholic. The family were forced to move to England, because neither Catholics nor Unionists were willing to accept and protect that sort of mixed marriage in the 1950s and 1960s: they would always be in danger in Belfast. That's the origin of Patrick's hatred of discrimination, which was so much a part of his style as a head. 'I still have relatives who have never met each other,' he told me. The family settled in the West Midlands, where he was brought up as a Catholic – the Catholic Church in those days would have excommunicated his mother if she had failed to promise this – although he describes himself as 'an Ulsterman, a Unionist, British, but very Irish'.

Patrick passed his eleven-plus. He told *The Tablet* in 2003 that this was

> unfortunate because I went to grammar school and hated every minute: the brutality, lack of care, love or kindness. It was at the time when Ugandan Asians were coming over and I was outraged by the racist abuse they had to endure from other students and indifference from staff. I would threaten people who threatened them.

He added in 2009, when he spoke to me: 'Those who failed the eleven-plus were marked as failures. Even those in the bottom half of the year at the grammar school were marked as failures.' From that comes his dislike of selection at the age of eleven and his desire to head a genuinely comprehensive school. 'Whatever you want you can achieve at a good community school,' he says.

And he married a black Londoner, a fellow teacher who is now a primary school head. He told *The Tablet* that visitors often ask her for the head teacher because they cannot believe such a senior post is filled by a black woman. His two children, now thirty and twenty-seven, have experienced discrimination: they look black, and his son has regularly been stopped in his car, though he has no criminal record. The same thing happens to Patrick's brother-in-law, a barrister with an expensive car. In a multicultural school like Cardinal Wiseman, it all helped him to identify with black parents anxious for their children to succeed.

Early on, he embraced liberation theology, which holds that salvation depends not only on avoiding individual sin, but also on fulfilling the aspirations of oppressed peoples and social classes. It achieved some success among progressive Catholics after the Second Vatican Council in the early 1960s. 'It gives me my inspiration,' he told me. 'We are building the Kingdom of God here and now. When you get up in the morning you are making the decision to involve yourself with the world.' None of this is likely to commend itself to the present Pope or the present Cardinal Archbishop of Westminster, which may be a part of his present troubles – but that is to jump ahead of ourselves.

Initially, Patrick taught mostly in deprived inner city areas in London – Harringay, Bethnal Green, Harlesden – and had already been a head teacher twice when he arrived at Cardinal Wiseman. But he knew at once it was the place he wanted to be. A large proportion of the 1,700 pupils were black. Many pupils were under-achieving, and the head could not walk round the school alone – he needed to be accompanied by a phalanx of teachers. He was sure he could change the under-achievement and the atmosphere. But he wanted to be sure he was not going to be undermined by his governors, and before he took the job he presented them with what he calls a covenant. This document, which the governors now say they cannot find, says:

Do not appoint me if you want to micro-manage me.
I need flexibility and full delegation on these issues:

› Staff development – power to promote and remove.
› A finance/business model for the school directly related to the best possible recruitment and retention (R&R) package for staff.
› Pattern of term times.

- › Flexibility in implementing government guidelines and priorities. 'Picking winners'.
- › Let me take calculated risks.
- › Good discipline.
- › Concentrate on outcomes KS2–KS4, do not get sidetracked on KS4.

'I needed to cut through all the bureaucracy,' he told me.

Getting the right staff was a priority, and Patrick was not prepared to wait until those teachers who he thought could not make the changes he wanted either retired or left of their own volition. He wanted them gone at once. Some of them, he says, were only interested in the top 20 per cent of the pupils. He offered a deal to the teachers he did not want. He told them that they were burned out and he needed their resignations straight away – but he would go on paying them for two terms. They could even come into school and sit in the staff room if they liked. In addition to getting better, more energetic teachers, this also enabled him to increase the proportion of ethnic minority teachers very quickly, which he considered important in a school with so many ethnic minority pupils. He managed very effectively to recruit and promote teachers from ethnic minorities. There were just three when he arrived in 1997, but within six years they made up almost a third of his 157 staff.

Patrick did not set out specifically to appoint ethnic minority teachers. He did, however, ask questions in interviews which tended to favour them. All applicants for jobs were asked what they thought about the under-achievement of black pupils, and about their opinion of the Macpherson report into the murder of the black teenager Stephen Lawrence, which found that there was institutional racism in the Metropolitan Police. If they did not know anything about it, or had no opinions on it, he did not think they would be much use at his school.

'More black teachers made a huge difference to the school,' he told me. 'It's a failing of Catholic schools – they have a low proportion of black teachers.' He says one black governor was made to feel unwelcome and was told: 'This is a white Irish school.' It's this sort of attitude, Patrick says, which led to the Catholic Church losing so many black people to the evangelical churches.

Teachers were the key, he says: 'Take away all the equipment and the money but leave the teachers and you will still have a great school.' Under Patrick, teachers find that they are allowed, even encouraged, to take calculated risks, and are not expected to be on the premises between set times. Success, he says, has nothing to do with time spent in school, it's to do with high expectations. He's happy to teach the national curriculum in four days and have the fifth day for enrichment – music, the Duke of Edinburgh's Award, sports coaching – or for targeting groups of students. 'I don't do "presenteeism",' he told the TES. 'If a teacher can do everything necessary by 3.30 p.m., so be it. I am an early morning person, but on a Friday at 3.30 p.m. I'm off to play football, and nothing stands in the way of that.'

On discipline Patrick had to act swiftly and decisively. He excluded twelve boys, blacks, whites and Asians among them, who were identified as key troublemakers. They were bullying others, and had formed gangs which created no-go areas on their estates. Following the initial purge, he did not need to use exclusion anything like as often, perhaps once a year. But a pupil who brings in a knife is expelled and can never return.

Before his first year at Cardinal Wiseman was over, examination results had improved and the school was a safer place. Patrick was able to do lunchtime duty on his own, and the school's GCSE pass rate went from 34 per cent to 50 per cent. For the rest of his time there, Patrick was out every lunchtime and at the end of the school day, when the head and other senior staff stand outside the school to ensure that pupils avoid muggers and drug dealers as they catch their buses home. They have had death threats and verbal abuse, and have even been assaulted. But Patrick carried on. He told the *Times Educational Supplement* in 2003: 'I walk the corridors, I do the stuff on the street. I am the figurehead, and pupils have regular contact with me. We have a full-time family educational therapist, we mentor, we listen, we coax.'

Being highly visible is very much his style. His door was always open, and pupils could drop in and ask him things. He had a reputation for being a good listener to pupils who came to him with grievances. He was a distinctive figure around the school, always sharply dressed and frequently wearing sunglasses. *The Tablet* found him in 2003 in a black pinstriped suit and a tie in shades of bright pink. He once asked a boy: 'What can I make you do to turn up to school?' The boy said: 'Give me one of your designer suits so I can wear it at the leavers' dance.' Patrick agreed, so long as the boy got five A–Cs, but the boy was a better bargainer than the head: he promised the five A–Cs if he got the suit upfront. So Patrick gave it to him, and the boy got six GCSEs, five of them A–Cs. 'It was a beautiful black suit with four buttons down the front,' says Patrick, a little wistfully. 'His life wasn't regular but he was intelligent. It became a standing joke, with boys pointing at my suit and saying "that's the suit I want, sir".'

Since his suspension the rumour mill has inevitably got to work on his designer suits, so he talked a little about them to me:

> Since I was a teenager, I've always liked nice clothes. As a teacher I think you should dress as smartly as you can. I have suits from Dolce and Gabbana, that sort of thing, but I'm careful about buying them. In the summer sales you can pick up a £1,000 suit for £200 and if you look after them they last six or seven years. I dress well, I'm co-ordinated, I look smart and sharp. But I have never insisted on it for the staff. I've never forced a dress code on them. So long as they do the job well I don't care what they wear.

Once the immediate battleground was cleared up, Patrick could set himself some long-term aims. He wanted especially to end under-achievement among black boys. At Cardinal Wiseman they analysed pupil progress by ethnicity and gender: white boys, Irish, Travellers and so on. Eight out of ten pupils come from an ethnic minority. 'Everybody wants the best for their child,' Patrick says. Often their background is very complicated. How does a mixed-race child determine his racial identity? Patrick thinks it's about making them comfortable with who they are, and that many of them define themselves as Londoners, black Londoners possibly, with a link to another country through their parents or their grandparents. His success with black children brought more applications from black families, but some white Catholic families have kept away, not wanting their children to go to what they think of as a black school.

Having been able to stop excluding pupils, Patrick became more relaxed about discipline. He reproached pupils rather than getting angry with them. He told them they were wasting time, missing out. He listened to their grievances, and they came to believe they would get justice and fair treatment from him. He told *The Tablet* in 2003: 'The major thing we do is talk to the children as though they were our own, as though they belonged to us. They know they matter to us. There is no time they come to you for help and you say "I don't have time".'

None of this was done without controversy. As head, Patrick made powerful enemies – perhaps more powerful than he knew. Whether that has any bearing on what happened in March 2009, we cannot know. But what we do know is that Paul Patrick the successful head, loved and admired in his school, is indistinguishable from Paul Patrick the controversialist, and that the first could not exist without the second.

First, there was the matter of admissions. Patrick is implacably opposed to any form of selection – not just the traditional selection by eleven-plus examination, which creates grammar schools and secondary moderns in some areas, or the traditional selection by wealth, but also the forms of selection which are common in Roman Catholic schools, and often in other faith schools. So, once he had restored Cardinal Wiseman's reputation, and the school started to be over-subscribed, he refused to conduct interviews of prospective pupils and their parents, which were traditionally used by Catholic school heads to select their pupils. He was delighted when Catholic schools were banned from doing this after 2003, though it was greeted with outrage by other Catholic heads. He told *The Tablet*:

As a Catholic I am ashamed of practices in other Catholic schools in London. I am ashamed to be a Catholic. The interviewing, the social selection! Option for the poor? Education for all? And we are Catholics! Local people are not able to get into their local secondary school because it has chosen to give places to bright middle-class kids from 10 miles away. It is a scandal. I am hoping the new admissions procedures will stop that dead.

There is no social or academic selection here. Black kids are achieving here. Ethnic minority kids are achieving here. Travellers are here. To us that is a complete contrast with other Catholic comprehensives.

For good measure he told the *Times Educational Supplement*:

I am still appalled and ashamed by some of the admissions procedures in Catholic schools nationally – the covert selection of more academic kids and the turning away of those with special needs. If one of the criteria is how often parents read in Mass, what chance does a single parent working in a supermarket in Southall have? In terms of liberation theology and options for the poor, I believe we are doing our bit here.

To determine whether applicants for places were practising Catholics, Cardinal Wiseman relied on a parish priest's reference. If two children had an equal claim, the school took the one who lived nearer. It all made Cardinal Wiseman a bit of a rogue elephant among Roman Catholic schools.

Just before Patrick was suspended, but while he was away, the governors made a change to the admissions arrangements which he had always opposed, designed to give greater priority to Catholics. They removed a clause which Patrick had always fiercely defended. The only reason the school had any non-Catholic children was that, before his arrival, it had been forced to take anyone, since it was under-subscribed. When it became

over-subscribed it started to take only Roman Catholic children.
But it still took siblings of existing or former non-Catholic pupils.
The idea was to keep faith with those families that had chosen
the school at its lowest ebb. The governors stopped this, and the
school now consists entirely, or almost entirely, of Roman Catholic
children. Whether this change had anything to do with subsequent
events it is impossible to say, but it is a change Patrick would have
fiercely opposed had he been there.

He's not impressed by government initiatives and directions
from on high, and is quite prepared to bin directives if they do not
suit him. 'If we have to abolish the timetable all week for a group
of kids to concentrate on science, we will do it,' he told the *TES*,
which interviewed him as part of a series on 'maverick heads'.
For the same article, Cardinal Wiseman's head of ethnic minority
achievement, Henderson Clark, said:

> Paul believes that everybody has to take risks if they want to do
> well, and even if you fail he will back you. The children have a
> voice, and access to him is the easiest thing in the world. I was
> with him at the end of one day when a youngster was going
> mad outside the school gate. I told him not to go, but he said
> he could not run away from it.
>
> He takes the idea of a Christian community seriously. If a
> girl gets pregnant, he has her back after she's had the baby. He
> would not cast her out. But if you are dealing drugs, you're out.
> He would know about you even before you put your hand in
> your pocket, because the children would tell him. They trust
> him totally, and they have good reason to do so.

Finally, there's Cuba – possibly the most controversial thing
even this controversial head has done, and, perhaps, the thing that
has brought him the most enemies.

In 2003 Patrick travelled to Cuba to see if it was possible
to form some sort of link with a school in the country. 'We'd
transformed the school so now we started to fill in the blanks,'
he says, and one of those blanks, for this most internationalist of

head teachers, was an international dimension. But why Cuba? 'It's safe there, we taught Spanish, and I had visited the country and had friends in education there,' he says. Was there a deep and dark political motive too? He says not, and I'm inclined to believe him. The story falls into the same category as the rumour, repeated in a national newspaper, that he kept a bust of Lenin in his office, which he didn't.

The first sixth-form group went to Cuba the next year, and links were developed with schools all over the country. What he calls the 'jewel in the crown' was the link with the San Alejandro Fine Arts Academy, founded in 1818, which has trained all the leading Cuban artists. Fee-charging schools all over Britain want a link with them, says Mr Patrick, but only Cardinal Wiseman has one.

Over the years two thirds of the staff – not just the teachers – have visited Cuba, as have hundreds of pupils; Cubans have visited Ealing; and Patrick has been able to take educational resources to Cuba that the American blockade has denied it. It was brave and imaginative, but it was also politically dangerous, earning Patrick an undeserved reputation as an extremist. Its contribution to what happened in March 2009 is, as I write in December 2009, impossible to assess.

What happened in March 2009 was this. On the day that Patrick arrived home from Cuba, he received a telephone call at home from Mike Pittendreigh, assistant director of education for the Roman Catholic Diocese of Westminster, asking him to come straight to the diocesan office: there were questions over his expenses. He was banned from going into his school.

Pittendreigh had advised the governors not to allow Patrick to enter the school, to prohibit him from contacting anyone 'associated with' the school, and to call the police. The police asked the chair of governors, Maggie Pound, whether she wanted a police investigation, or whether they would investigate themselves; Pound opted for the police, on Pittendreigh's advice.

So Patrick kicked his heels at home for a month waiting for something to happen, and on 21 April it did. At 7 a.m. a posse of policemen, some of them from the Fraud Squad, arrived at his home, searched it thoroughly and took him to the police station. He was eventually given police bail.

The police told him they were looking for anything on Havana Experience, the organisation he created to run the Cuba exchanges, and he has told friends he gave them all he had. No money went through Havana Experience and it never traded. They suggested he had channelled money to a former school employee now living in Poland. He says the money was her severance pay, and was sent by the school bursar. There was a suggestion that he had used Building Schools for the Future money on the Cuban exchange, which he says is quite untrue. They said he had travelled to Cuba business class, thereby wasting public money; he says he travelled business class because he was taking boxes of educational materials, and a business class passenger had 100 kilograms of luggage allowance, so it was cheaper that way.

The police interviewed him again in June, and eventually, in August, released him from bail and said there would be no charges. Then Patrick met Pittendreigh and Pound. Although the governors had opted for a police investigation, they now decided to mount their own, saying they were conducting an audit of his expenses and were appointing another Catholic school head to investigate Patrick's leadership and management of the school. They dismissed the police's refusal to bring charges, saying that the head had not been found innocent – all the police had done was to say there was not sufficient evidence.

The main charges still related to the Cuban exchange. This is something Patrick is immensely proud of. Now the link is suspended – the pupils who should have gone to Cuba in February 2010 did not go. The only Cuban exchange in a British state school looks like being a casualty of the affair.

Patrick ran the link – and the school – with a level of freedom which most head teachers would envy. His friends say that he did it all according to a covenant he agreed with the governors when he was first appointed, giving him an exceptional level of autonomy – the covenant quoted above. One long-standing governor, Professor David Foskett of Thames Valley University, was on the panel that appointed Patrick and remembers the covenant clearly. 'We gave him carte blanche to turn the school round,' he says. 'We needed to give him enough freedom to manage it. We gave him that in writing.'

The covenant, say Patrick's friends, was in both his personal file and the governors' file, and if he had been allowed into his office when he returned from Cuba, he could have produced it. They say it has mysteriously gone missing. I asked Pound about it, and her carefully worded reply was emailed to me: 'No written covenant between Mr Patrick and the governing body has been found to exist.'

As I write, in December 2009, Patrick has been suspended on full pay for nearly eight months, and there is no sign of a resolution. His friends insist there is a vendetta, though they are divided about whose vendetta it is. Wilder theories include a plot by Cuban exiles to discredit a man who is providing aid for education in communist Cuba. Others point out that the new Cardinal Archbishop of Westminster, Vincent Nichols, is known to be keen to bring Catholic schools under greater central control, and strong heads such as Patrick get in the way. They also mention that changes to the school admission criteria which give greater priority for Catholics, opposed by Patrick, have now been implemented.

Another factor may be the troubled past shared by Patrick and Pittendreigh. Pittendreigh had been head of a failing school and Patrick was a member of the interim board appointed to manage it; Pittendreigh left the job. 'Did this make Pittendreigh an inappropriate person to handle Patrick's case?' I asked Pound, who replied: 'When I contacted the diocese I was not aware of Mr Pittendreigh's former employment, but have valued and have full confidence in the advice and guidance he has offered the governors.' No one has complained, she added.

Whatever is going on, the cost to the public purse is mounting, and a head whom everyone, on all sides, calls inspirational, is doing no useful work and is becoming ill from stress and worry. Pound defends the long delay, claiming that the governors could not investigate until the police investigation was over: 'I am unable to determine how long any investigation which might be required will take, but can give an assurance that matters will be attended to as promptly as possible.'

But Professor Foskett thinks it has gone on far too long already. When the police investigation ended, he sent an email to all governors demanding Patrick's reinstatement. The diocese's director of education, Paul Barber, wrote to him accusing him of breaching governors' confidentiality. Foskett resigned from the governing body in disgust. 'Paul Patrick is a dynamic leader. They need him back in the school,' he says.

The diocese, having advised Pound all along in her decisions to call in the police, mount an investigation, ban the head from entering his school and all the rest, is now leaving her alone to deal with the fallout. Its press officer at first offered to arrange an interview for me with the official who played a key role in Patrick's suspension, but twenty-four hours later he changed his mind and refused even to give me the official's name. I had to find out for myself that the official is Mr Pittendreigh, who seems to have been the key player in Patrick's downfall. Pound was left in the unenviable position of defending everything that had been done without any support from the diocese.

And Pound's position is complicated by that of her husband, local MP Steve Pound. Their children attended the school and Mr Pound used to visit it regularly. Now, in another written statement, Mrs Pound told me: 'Steve Pound has no formal connection with the school, he is no longer a parent of a pupil, nor is he a governor and the school is not in his constituency.' But it is just the other side of the constituency boundary and a great many of its families are Mr Pound's constituents.

No one wants to know the school, or to be associated with it. But until March 2009, everyone – the Catholic hierarchy, Steve Pound MP – wanted to know Paul Patrick and bathe in his reflected glory.

*

Stop press: Paul Patrick, seriously ill from stress, resigned on
22 January 2010. Details of the settlement he reached with
the governors are secret, but his National Union of Teachers
representative said:

> We are absolutely certain that he could have cleared his name
> of any financial or other wrongdoing had he had the chance to
> do so. Paul Patrick has made no personal gain from the public
> finances of his school, and has managed its financial affairs
> no differently in the last year to the previous twelve years,
> when budgets were submitted to and scrutinised by governors
> in the proper manner . . . What has changed, however, seems
> to have been the governors' faith in his leadership. This is
> their prerogative, but could have been managed far more
> professionally without the prolonged distress that has been
> caused to everyone associated with the school's community.

On 10 February the governors made public their investigation
and drew journalists' attention to the head's first-class airline
flights. His name has finally been removed from the school's
website, but his achievements remain there.

Sean O'Regan
Not *a* head teacher,
the head of Edith Neville School

When I saw him in December 2009, Sean O'Regan had a victory
to celebrate. The man who never wanted to be a head – he still
misses classroom teaching – has been in the eye of one of London
education's biggest political storms, and has discovered hitherto
unsuspected subtlety in the dark arts of politics.

O'Regan is the head of Edith Neville primary school in
Somers Town, in the London Borough of Camden. Its cramped
building lies, forgotten and unloved, behind the gleaming new St
Pancras station and the British Library. Unloved, that is, by local
planners and business folk, but not by those who use it. Somers
Town itself is described by Wendy Wallace in a book about the
school as 'a dense and parochial urban village with old council
houses all around it'. The decaying social housing near the
school has a high proportion of Bangladeshi families – they are
the second biggest ethnic group in the area, after white British,
and the white British are generally older. Edith Neville School
has a much higher proportion of Bangladeshi children than the
area itself, because there are three faith schools just a street or
two away – a Church of England primary, and Roman Catholic
junior and infant schools. These, whose admissions criteria favour
Christians, take most of the white children and a high proportion
of the black African ones. In Camden as a whole, the majority of
primary schools are Christian faith schools. Thirteen of them are
Church of England and eight are Roman Catholic; the remaining
twenty are non-faith. 'The Anglican vicar here has fewer than 20

children in church on Sunday but more than 200 in his school,'
says O'Regan.

So there is huge pressure on places in schools where Muslim
(or, for that matter, Buddhist, Hindu or atheist) children can feel
at home, and where they are not actively kept out by admissions
criteria which demand Christian observance. Edith Neville School
is very strict about admitting those who live closest to it – 'This is
a community school,' says O'Regan – to the extent that his own
two older children, who attended the nursery, did not get a place
in Reception, and in 2009, aged eight and six, were attending
a primary school nearer their home.

The result is that an Edith Neville classroom is a colourful
collection of headscarves. One of O'Regan's classes has 100
per cent Muslim children. Fifty-five per cent of the intake is
Bangladeshi in origin. The next biggest group is Somali.

Most of his professional life has gone into the school. 'I'm not
a head teacher, I'm *the* head teacher of Edith Neville School,' he
says. So when he perceived a threat to it, he was ready to fight
tooth and nail. The threat came, indirectly, from plans to build a
spanking new academy on the other side of the borough – in Swiss
Cottage, the wealthy bit of Camden. Edith Neville School was
going to be collateral damage.

One of the two buildings that needed to make way for the
academy, sponsored by University College London (UCL), housed
the Frank Barnes School for deaf children. 'They looked at all
the sites available for a land grab and saw Edith Neville, with
some land and serving the most deprived children in the borough.
So they said, "Let's stick Frank Barnes there too."' Land is much
less valuable in Somers Town than in Swiss Cottage.

The idea was to rebuild Edith Neville School and make the
building big enough to accommodate Frank Barnes School, and
the two schools would work together. It made sense in planning
terms, but none at all in educational terms, says O'Regan. 'We
have twenty-six spoken languages here. If we added fully signing
language to that, it would be bad for all the children. Deaf
children, if they do not have their own school, would do better in

a school where English was generally the first language.' He took
councillors to see his nursery class, in which no child had English
as their first language. Deaf children in that class, learning to
sign, would add yet another language to an already complicated
linguistic mix, he told them.

But he was not offered a choice. In 2007 Camden Council
decided to go ahead with the merger. O'Regan recalls a councillor
in 2007, 'sitting', he said, 'where you're sitting now' in his office,
and saying to him: 'It's a forced marriage. Make it work.' For
nothing was to stand in the way of the new academy. UCL
was easily the most prestigious university to agree to sponsor
(though not pay for) one of the government's academies, and it is
believed to have been personally brought into the project by the
then schools minister, Lord Adonis. It was a prominent part of
the government's academy programme, in which ministers have
invested a huge amount of political capital.

To keep the project alive, the government and Camden
Council were forced to fight a legal battle; for the choice of UCL
as sponsor was challenged in the courts and fought by a group
of Camden parents and teachers under the banner of CASE,
the Campaign for State Education. They attacked the rather
obscure process by which UCL had been chosen as sponsor.
Kevin Courtney, branch secretary of Camden National Union
of Teachers, summed up their concerns:

> We want UCL to share their expertise with all Camden schools
> and not just the chosen few in their school, which is situated
> on one of the most exclusive streets in London. We fear that
> the school will cream off the brightest students and this will
> damage other Camden schools and therefore have a negative
> effect on education overall.

Camden Council was prepared to brave criticisms of its choice
of the Swiss Cottage site, which was itself controversial. While
Swiss Cottage is wealthy, the south of the borough, which includes
Edith Neville, is poor and much less well supplied with secondary

schools. All nine of the borough's existing secondary schools lie north of Euston Road, the road on which sit Euston, King's Cross and St Pancras stations and the British Library. And the Swiss Cottage site is just a few hundred yards from Quintin Kynaston School, though QK is over the border in the City of Westminster. QK is a well-regarded and successful school whose head teacher, Jo Shuter, has been Head Teacher of the Year and is one of the heads profiled in this book.

On top of this lie all the normal objections to academies. They are owned and controlled by their sponsors, and not by the community – UCL will appoint a majority of the fifteen governors at its academy. The UCL top brass believe in uniforms and an extended school day, and although they say they will not micromanage the school, there is no doubt that their academy will feature both.

So UCL had started wondering whether the game was worth the candle before it had even heard of Sean O'Regan. Professor Michael Worton, UCL vice provost and the man leading the academy project, told the *Times Educational Supplement*: 'We hadn't realised just how much time it was going to take. We have built a lot of buildings over the past decade but we have never had a process that is quite so onerous.' Would they have gone into the project if they had understood the problems? 'It is a question I have posed. We would certainly have reflected longer.'

O'Regan campaigned vigorously against having the Frank Barnes School dumped on him – not just for the sake of his school but, he insists, for the sake of Frank Barnes as well. Eventually he took the extreme step of notifying the council that Edith Neville was considering applying for foundation status. This is the first move away from being a local authority school, and it is not a direction in which O'Regan – a firm believer in community schools – is temperamentally inclined to travel. But the law requires that as soon as a school has notified the local education authority that it is considering foundation status, the authority is barred from making any changes to its status. That stops Camden Council from relocating another school onto the site.

So the move was stymied, perhaps to the quiet relief of both UCL and Camden, who had enough enemies already without adding O'Regan and his loyal and vociferous parents and governors to their number. It has now been quietly withdrawn. The academy project has been rescued with a different solution. Frank Barnes is to stay where it is, but will be combined with the other school on the site. This is the Jack Taylor School, an all-age community special school for pupils with severe learning difficulties and with profound and multiple needs. The merged school will share some facilities with the academy. This merger, too, has provoked opposition from parents, although it remains to be seen how far this opposition will hold things up; it may prove easier to steamroller than that at Edith Neville School.

It's a victory for O'Regan, no doubt about it, but he has learned too much about politics while achieving it to gloat over his defeated opponent, and will not be drawn on his views about the academy proposal. His concern now is to get a new building, which he will no longer have to share, with funds from the Primary Capital Programme, the government's fund for rebuilding or refurbishing primary schools.

It's urgent. He is working in a building that is supposed to accommodate 155 children, and he has 262. People are desperate to get their children into the school, so only those who live closest get in, and he has to stretch the rules even to take children who live a few streets away. Having Ofsted rave about the place ('Edith Neville Primary is an outstanding school, which makes a really positive difference to pupils' skills, aspirations and life chances. The outstanding leadership, teaching and learning and an exciting curriculum, contribute to pupils' success . . .') is almost an embarrassment, not just because it increases the pressure on places, but because it weakens his argument for a new building and more space. You're doing so well that you could hardly do better even with a splendid new building, runs the argument. In science, almost all pupils already reach the higher Level 5 in national tests. In 2007, the school was in the top 4 per cent nationally for adding value to pupils' attainment. How could you do better with a bit

more money? But we could, says O'Regan, and he has presented
Camden Council with a document showing how it could be done.

'We are top of the list for the next tranche of money,' O'Regan
told me hopefully in December 2009. But he is also a realist, and
he knows that he has to wait for his money until April 2011,
by which time there will be a new government and there may still
be an economic crisis; and huge quantities of public funding will
have gone into the UCL academy, which will make it harder for
Camden to make a case for more building money. Sixteen months
is an eternity in politics.

He knows it will help make his case if the school is central
to community regeneration; and anyway, that's what he wants.
So in April 2009 Edith Neville hosted a conference designed to
find and fund ways of regenerating the very poor area in which it
is situated, and it has been central in the production of a brochure
called *New Heart for Somers Town*. O'Regan is determined that
Somers Town should not be left out of the area's new-found
wealth – the new UCL research centre being built beside the
British Library and the new St Pancras International station.

The brochure says:

> In recent months design and architecture journals and the film
> titled *Somers Town* have raised the area's profile nationally
> against the background of major development nearby. There
> is a great love of Somers Town and strong local feelings that
> it must remain Somers Town through any changes – but
> change will happen . . . How can we build on change and the
> strengths of Somers Town to the benefit of the area and its
> communities?
>
> This multicultural residential enclave, closed in between
> Euston and St Pancras stations on the north side of Euston
> Road, faces significant issues – for example around poor
> health and housing . . . Long-awaited development of the
> immediately adjacent King's Cross Central is starting,
> redevelopment along Euston Road is afoot, plans for Euston
> station, west of Euston, north of the British Library and

St Pancras Hospital are progressing. How can development have positive impacts – physically, socially and economically – on Somers Town's communities?

Within Somers Town itself there is investment currently proposed in school rebuilding that provides a once-in-a-lifetime opportunity to rethink the 'old heart' of the area. How can the investment and design achieve added value in terms of providing what the community needs and wants alongside and within its new schools?

In addition to neighbouring development, Somers Town has a growing number of nationally and internationally ranking facilities on its doorstep – St Pancras International, University College London, the Wellcome Trust, the British Library and the future site for Central St Martin's. How can they engage with its communities in ways that can change aspiration and economic potential rather than causing displacement? . . . At a time when resources are increasingly scarce this approach, of looking at potential gains from development projects within and around the area, is pragmatic.

Schools such as Edith Neville could be central to the regeneration of the area.

With five schools in the area, youth can be readily accessed. Close by are national institutions – Westminster Kingsway College, University College London, the Institute of Education and soon Central St Martin's – that should come together to work with the youth of Somers Town. This could be an action research project in showing how education in its broadest sense can work to raise aspiration and overcome deprivation. Mentoring programmes, work experience and training could easily be increased and made more accessible through a 'sorting office'. Outreach work as part of degree and further education courses could take part in the community. Schools are very bogged down . . . and they don't have time to make the links with other organisations that they might like to.

This thinking came from O'Regan's own contribution to the conference. He said that it was

> crucial that schools receive support or funding to carry out this work with the community. A co-ordinator/dedicated community engagement manager could work with all the schools in the area. Schools provide a direct link to communities through the children and increasingly through parent classes and children's centres for the 0–3-year-olds. The exceptional number of schools in the centre of Somers Town include some that are very outward looking and with a strong ethos of involving their communities.

He drew on Edith Neville's own experience to tell his colleagues:

> Drawing in parents from wider community resources has huge impacts on children's outcome. So the good schools aren't just about children; they are also about the adults who don't just come in and drop children off for classes . . . We have adult education classes, we have ICT, skills in accessing employment, all as part of the fabric of what we do.
>
> For too long now schools have not been set up for any more than the business and work of pedagogy – the craft of teaching that goes on in the classroom. If schools are truly enabled to look outward to their communities then they are in a vital place. So there's a potential there . . . to be a beating heart for positive change.

So putting money into Edith Neville isn't just about improving the education that children get there. The brochure concludes that 'the rebuilding of the two community schools offers a once-in-a-lifetime opportunity to reconfigure the area nearby and provide more of what communities need and want. What is currently an assortment of municipal spaces could become, with strategic planning, a place of general pride and enjoyment.'

O'Regan told me: 'Schools can be agents for regenerating communities. We are a little back street primary school but so much is happening here. It's a very poor neighbourhood and we have to make sure it's not left to rot.' Apart from teaching children, the school is being used to train women from the Bangladeshi community to be child minders, so that others can go out to work. 'The forced marriage was a big distraction from all this,' says O'Regan.

The reason Edith Neville is heavily over-subscribed is partly because the other nearby primaries are Christian faith schools, partly because of its top results and splendid Ofsted reports, and partly because it has standard admissions criteria and does not skew its intake towards Christians. But there's another reason, and you have to go there to see it. Despite the poverty, despite the cramped conditions, it's as happy a school as you could wish to see, and relationships between pupils and staff are easy and natural.

There is no uniform, and children call teachers by their first name. It's fashionable today to sneer at this way of working as a relic of the 1960s, but it works perfectly well: children do not run riot because they are expected to call the head 'Sean'. The two poised and confident ten-year-old girls who showed me round, Suban and Yasmya, found it quite natural to tell me that the Year 4 teacher is called Dave, but 'when we were in Year 4 we had a teacher called Nick'.

When the governors decided against uniforms, O'Regan, unusually, did not offer any views, but he does say now: 'People think a uniform is a short cut to raising standards of behaviour, but it is not.' The local church schools have uniforms, which causes some parents to see them as a cut above Edith Neville, 'but', says O'Regan with pardonable complacency, 'this is not borne out by the results'. In what had been a very traditionally run school, he wanted to bring in a child-friendly culture and raise standards at the same time.

What difference does it make? I saw that quite early in my visit. As soon as I arrived, O'Regan took me past a line of six-year-olds waiting patiently for the instruction to enter a classroom, and a little girl in a red headscarf threw her arms round him and said: 'Sean, I'm missing you.' She had probably last seen him the previous day. For many of these children, school is an oasis of calm in their lives. Many of them arrive in the care of uncles; they are waiting for the rest of their family to get permission to join them here. Some have been in war zones, and have dreadful memories which will never be erased. Some arrive with almost no education. O'Regan recalled for me a nine-year-old, just arrived from Peshawar, who had never seen a computer, and when a teacher gave her a pencil, she had no idea what to do with it. Her father explained that she had not been to school before.

How does Edith Neville cope with a nine-year-old who has had no schooling at all? 'The other children were falling over themselves to help her. My staff are very diverse and speak a great many languages, and we use volunteers from UCL to teach languages.' I watched a little boy of nine interpreting for two new children. 'A child like that will arrive scared and lonely,' says O'Regan. Yet, because of her age, her performance in Key Stage 2 tests counts when the school's results are shown. 'I don't know how this serves her learning needs as a young child.' O'Regan refuses to be what he calls a SATs (Standard Assessment Tests) factory.

This head teacher is utterly committed to this school and no other. When he says 'I'm not a head teacher, I'm the head teacher of Edith Neville School' it's literally true. In 2009 he marked his twentieth year there, starting as a classroom teacher, and he never wanted to be a head – he still misses being a classroom teacher. Sometimes O'Regan sounds as though he still wishes he could go back to being a class teacher, and I am sure at least a part of him does. 'I stopped being a teacher when I became head and started to be a fundraiser,' he says.

O'Regan was born in 1964 in rural Cork, but his parents soon moved to Jersey, where he attended the primary school of which is mother was head teacher. He was an academic high flyer. He got fourteen O-levels at his Roman Catholic boys' school, took an Oxford degree and a Reading University teaching qualification, and went to Edith Neville as a 26-year-old class teacher in 1990, although his mother and grandmother warned him off teaching as a career. At that time he was both a Christian and a socialist, and felt strongly that he wanted to work among the poor. He was also interested, academically, in pedagogy. The school has been his adult life. Seven years later, he was its head, when it was at the bottom of the borough's league tables.

It happened like this. The previous head resigned, and the deputy head died suddenly. O'Regan was made acting head. Ofsted inspectors were expected, and the building was subsiding. The governors advertised the headship three times, and each time O'Regan refused to apply; he was living for the day he could get back to being the class teacher of Year 3. But eventually he agreed to apply, and with a sigh of relief they appointed him.

He started dating his future wife, Nasima Rashid, when he was a class teacher at Edith Neville and she came to teach there, though they had first met when they were both doing Master's degrees at the Institute of Education in Bloomsbury, a few hundred yards but a whole continent away from Edith Neville School. At first they had to keep their burgeoning relationship secret from colleagues, and from her family; they met once a week, a long way from the school. Even today Nasima's conservative Muslim family does not approve of the marriage, and the rift has not yet healed.

She is now the assistant head, and was acting head for the summer term of 2007. The youngest of their three children had just been born, and Mr O'Regan asked for a sabbatical to stay at home for a term to look after him.

He is slightly built, and talks fast and with animation, but quietly. The education journalist Wendy Wallace spent six months at Edith Neville School, and wrote her 2005 book *Oranges and Lemons: Life in an Inner City Primary School* about it. She warned me: 'You will not find it easy to keep Sean to one subject.' She was right. Words and ideas tumble out of him all the time. I only had a short time to spend at the school, and he wanted to tell me everything. He is as excited about it as though he only came to it yesterday.

Wallace's book chronicled the small meannesses required to keep the school going on inadequate public money:

> This year the amount they have to spend is down in real terms by about £100,000. 'Please pay Joan for your personal phone calls,' reads a notice on her wall. But the minor economies in place all over the school – staff paying for their own tea, coffee and personal photocopying, buying materials for projects out of their own pocket – are not enough. They have balanced the books this year by not replacing a departing teacher whose job was supporting children with English as a second language.

She recorded some of the human misery the staff saw and catalogued heartbreaking stories:

> Later in the day the head will be attending a child protection conference, he tells his staff. A couple are applying to have their daughter removed from the at-risk register. 'She's still covered in bruises,' interrupts a teacher, clearly upset. 'She's still dirty. Still hungry.' Her mobile phone goes off inside her bag and she reaches down into it with both hands, flustered ... A child in the juniors attempted suicide. Others face deportation, or go home after school to scenes of violence and despair.

It's all true, yet O'Regan felt that Wallace's book made the school sound too unremittingly bleak. 'You can see for yourself that this is a happy place,' he said to me. I could, but to understand the magnitude of his achievement, you have to see the school through Wallace's eyes. And in his next sentence, he seemed to be admitting that Wallace's picture was, at least in part, an inconvenient truth: 'Male life expectancy in Somers Town is eleven years younger than in Fitzjohns [where O'Regan lives], which is just 1½ miles away. But I don't want the children to know that.'

The school struggles with its building. During some construction work, they uncovered the foundation stone of the first school on that site, which dates it at 1874, but that school – which looks in pictures like a pretty substantial two-storey Victorian school building – was torn down in summer 1972, when Margaret Thatcher was education secretary, because it had only outside lavatories (it is not clear why they could not simply build lavatories inside), and the present building was thrown up in the summer vacation, in time for pupils to arrive that September. It was built to last twenty-five years, and is now well into its third decade.

It has given some awkward moments, and none more so than when O'Regan first became acting head in 1997. 'On my third day as acting head, the school started to fall down,' he says. The school borrowed a disused Victorian building normally used as council offices until theirs could be made safe. Governors lobbied the council then for a new building, but got the old one underpinned instead. When they returned from their temporary accommodation they found a leaking roof and wrecked playground. Over the next few years, O'Regan fundraised for, and oversaw the construction of, a remodelled interior. The arrival of Sure Start in Camden and the regeneration of King's Cross brought in some extra money, but it dried up before a new library could be built.

The building was completely open plan, and has had to be divided into working spaces. Every inch of space seems to be in use all the time – a lesson was being conducted in what looked to me like the corridor outside the head's office, though the space was clearly used to playing host to learning. The rather small and tatty school hall has pupils crammed into it for assembly, lunch and PE. There is no library, the roof still leaks, some of the walls are cracked, but the place looks bright, cheerful and welcoming.

The environment isn't a healthy one – Somers Town is low-lying and surrounded by major roads and railway stations, a natural pollution trap. Money had to be found for high perimeter railings, because the grounds were being used by the many prostitutes who work from King's Cross, and needles and condoms were being found all over the bushes.

O'Regan and his governors are painfully aware that many of his children come from very shabby homes, and want to make the school environment as good as they can. The new building is urgently needed.

He did manage to get some funding to build a nursery. In line with his determination to make the school very open to parents, O'Regan got the architects to build an ante-room by the nursery with one-way glass in it, so that worried parents could watch their children on their first days in the school and feel reassured. Many Bangladeshi women leave school at twelve, says Mr O'Regan, and schools are strange and frightening places for them.

It's hard to put your finger on exactly what O'Regan does that works, and I suspect it's as much the aura he gives off as anything. Nasima says it has something to do with involving children in decision-making – 'they feel valued and listened to'. It's also something to do with involving parents all the way – this is not one of those primary schools where parents feel unwanted if they stay with their children beyond the school gate.

One way of involving parents and engendering the feel of a community school is to employ some of them. At one time seven pupils in the school had a parent working there. Sometimes a parent is employed as a bilingual teaching assistant. They tend to be mothers who start out as volunteers and end up working at the school. It certainly also helps that the school has a fully trained reading recovery teacher, shared with one other school. Reading recovery was developed at Auckland University in New Zealand by Professor Marie Clay, and is the only method known to help children who have real difficulty learning to read. It detects reading difficulties at the age of six, and provides a child with individual tuition for half an hour every day for up to twenty weeks from a specially trained teacher, so it is very expensive. All the studies show that it works better than anything else yet discovered. It gets children up to the average level of reading for their age, and the knowledge sticks. A child who has been through reading recovery is extremely unlikely to grow up illiterate.

O'Regan is not the first head to testify that it works. The day I was there, Year 1 – six-year-olds – were rehearsing for their performance of *The Gruffalo*, and four of the children in the show had been through reading recovery.

Angela Palin
The head and the Renaissance man

If they gave awards to head teachers with an unerring instinct for recruiting Renaissance men and women, it would be easy to see why Angela Palin was Primary Head Teacher of the Year in 2009. Within half an hour of arriving at her tiny Cornish village school I had chatted to Rob and Hayley.

Rob is Renaissance man. He started his association with St Mellion School when he and his fifteen-seat minibus won the Cornwall Council contract to transport children there. He got on really well with the children on his bus, built up a rapport with them, and helped one or two who were having trouble with their friendships or just feeling miserable. Now, when he drives them to the school, he parks his minibus outside, brings his passengers in, and transforms himself into an assistant teacher, which is how he spends his mornings. Then there's another driving job before he has to go and keep an eye on another school where he's a part-time caretaker. He also runs the school chess club.

Hayley is Renaissance woman. She's a teaching assistant in the mornings, then a lunchtime supervisor (Palin doesn't believe in teachers supervising lunch), then she updates the school website.

By now it will come as no surprise that Jo, the school secretary, teaches cycling proficiency, and half the teaching staff take all fifty-nine pupils once a week to the swimming pool in the local golf club and teach them to swim. And that there was a mother in the school all day when I was there, filling in for an absent teacher, and other mothers teach netball, offer all sorts of other skills, and pop in and out of the school throughout the day.

'Everyone is so willing to offer the children everything they have got,' says Palin. 'I do see potential for people to bring other skills and put them in the pot. Parents want to keep on doing it. I just have to be around and be grateful. In a bigger school the head might not know what people can offer. We have an open door policy; parents can come in at any time.'

This is one of the skills that the council has persuaded her to extend to other schools in the area. Throughout 2009 she was also executive head of another local school a few miles away, Quethiock School, which was having great trouble finding a suitable new head. Now they have found one, Palin is becoming executive head of St Mellion and also of another local school in the next door village of St Dominick, St Dominic School (the village has a K at the end of its name but the school does not.)

Angela Palin is a tall, exuberant woman with that special brand of noisy, infectious, larger-than-life jollity that you find in many successful primary school teachers. You don't so much walk through her small school with her as get dragged along in her slipstream. When you find out that, after seven years, she started to feel St Mellion alone might be too small for her, you wonder what took her so long.

After taking a Bachelor of Education degree at Christchurch College, Canterbury, in 1980, she taught in Kent for ten years and had two sons before moving to Fowey in Cornwall, where she worked part time and looked after her children, and almost despite herself found that she was moving up the career ladder. For fairly soon, officials at Cornwall County Council had her marked out as someone of personality and ability who might be the human solution to some of their problem schools. One of these was St Mellion, which Ofsted diagnosed in 2001 as having serious weaknesses, and where the head was off sick. Palin never particularly wanted to be a head – she's not that ambitious, she says – but she came in as acting head in January 2002, and was appointed head teacher a year later when it became clear that her predecessor's illness was going to prevent her from coming back.

By 2007 Ofsted was raving about the place. 'Six years ago it had serious weaknesses and an uncertain future,' said the report. 'Two years later, the weaknesses had been resolved and sound foundations laid. Since then, strong and very effective leadership and the concerted efforts of everyone involved have seen the school go from strength to strength. Parents are delighted with the education their children receive.'

How did she do it? Ask most heads who have turned round their schools that question and there is a pat, ready-made answer, sometimes almost too neat. But not with Palin. She goes silent for a moment, as though it's not a question she has given a lot of thought to before. Unusually, she had not until recently taken a course in headship – she got the job just before it became compulsory – and I think she has succeeded as a head partly because she is quick, intuitive and likes people, both adults and children; and people respond to that. The process was less cerebral than with some other heads.

When she does reply, the first thing she says is the last thing I expected to hear. 'I had very good support from the county. They had a strong input into the action plan. They gave me a tailor-made induction for the job.' And that's a very surprising thing to say, because she is, without affectation or bombast, flying in the face of all the thinking of the last twenty years, all the nostrums of the Thatcher and Blair eras, in which local councils were cast as the force of reaction, holding back school improvement. Government ministers, companies and churches have cast themselves as the liberators, dragging schools out from under the dead weight of council bureaucracy. The idea that the successful head owes a debt to the local authority sounds extraordinary.

But she means it. She has found Cornwall a great support, partly, she says, because its education department officials tend to stay in their jobs, and there is continuity.

Of course, there is more to her success than intuition and good local authority support. It's not always easy for a head in her situation to talk publicly about what was wrong before she arrived, for it is hard to do so without seeming to attack people who do not deserve to be attacked, and for whom there is still affection. 'Hero heads', who like to make everything before their regime sound terrible in order to maximise their own achievement, do not mind upsetting the decaying remnants of the *ancien régime*, but Palin is not one of these. She says of the era before she arrived: 'The school was well liked and parents were not fazed by the poor Ofsted. They valued it for what it was. It is very small and they liked that.' However, it is clear she thinks that, immediately before her arrival, the school had not been led from the front.

One thing she changed radically was the building. Outside, this typical small nineteenth-century rural school – it was built in 1891 – looks just as it does in the aerial photograph they keep on the wall, which was taken fifty years ago. But the play area outside, with its lavish equipment, is new, paid for partly by the Parent–Staff Association (PSA). Inside, the building has been divided up – the main entrance used to lead into a classroom, but now it leads into a hallway. And it's been brightened up – it used to be oppressively dark. The old kitchen was demolished and a new one built. There are many more separate spaces. Next Palin wants a hall.

She talks of how she built a relationship with staff, pupils and parents, and as the children come into the school, you can see what she means about the parents. Many of them come in with their children, and Palin knows them all – their families, their illnesses, their lives. The school is, as she says, 'first and foremost a community school'. She made the school day longer, and ensured that an assembly was held every day.

For all this, and for all her loyalty to Cornwall Council, St Mellion could, under a different head, be something very different, for it is a church school, independent of the local authority and of the community. It can set its own admissions criteria. It does; but it sets them so as to remain as far as possible a community school. If it is over-subscribed – and it always is these days, having been under-subscribed before Palin's arrival – it takes siblings of existing pupils, then those in the designated area around the school, then those who have expressed a religious conviction. But the village of St Mellion is an ageing community, so despite these criteria there are only six children, from just three families, who could walk to school. Other pupils come from nearby towns of Saltash and Callington, for the school is on the main road, easy to get to, and has a good local reputation. There is a bus for nearby villages and farms, driven, naturally, by Rob.

This year, though the published admissions number – the number of new pupils the school is supposed to be able to accommodate – was eight, the governors decided to take ten children, so as not to turn away anybody who fulfilled any one of these three criteria. The result is a very mixed intake, including children from well-heeled professionals but with one in ten – six children – poor enough to qualify for free school meals. (It does not, of course, have any of the ethnic mix you find in city schools. I spotted just one black child, and he, it turned out, was a temporary pupil, in Britain for two months with his mother before returning to Africa.)

There are just two classes, where a bigger school would have seven. One class has, broadly, the 5–7-year-olds (Reception and Years 1 and 2) and the other has the 7–11-year-olds (Years 3 to 6). So in each class, with thirty or so children, teachers have to cope with a huge range of knowledge and ability. It's a challenge, though made easier by having more staff per child than you would get in a bigger primary school – I saw four adults in one classroom. Palin has two full-time teachers and three part-timers, as well as Rob and Hayley. There is not a lot of whole-class teaching, and they manage to keep in touch with the progress of children at several different levels. Groups of children are set different work, and teaching assistants are deployed to help the different groups.

The advantage is that children do not have to work in fixed year groups. Ability can be taken into account as well. Palin says:

> It becomes crucial that you know where each child is at. It is not as easy to fall off the end as it might be in a bigger school. We are able to work at an individual level. When I taught bigger year groups you would not always know the little things

that it pleases children you know. Behavioural problems are
easier to deal with here. Often when children misbehave they
are shouting for attention, and they don't have to shout very
loud to get noticed here. Children know each other and respect
each other because it is a small school. All the staff know
all the children. In September these children have the same
classroom and the same teachers as before. It's one big push
when they move up a class.

In that upper class we have thirty-six children, ranging
from seven year olds whose attainment is below the national
average to ten-year-olds almost off to secondary school.
The children do not think of themselves in conventional year
groups.

The key to making it work is people. They matter much more
than facilities. 'Our governors have always put money into staff,'
says Palin.

The size of the school affects the way she chooses teachers:

I look for someone who is not fazed by the idea of teaching a
whole key stage. They need a thorough understanding of the
whole of the national curriculum. They need to be more than
just a class teacher, because of those whole-school aspects. They
need to be able to engage with parents and the whole school
community.

The size of the school does make it a big wrench when the
children have to leave and go to a big secondary school. But they
have the advantage of one supportive secondary school, Callington
Community College, which most of them go to and which takes
children from several small village schools in the area. While
still at St Mellion, they go to the college's sports centre and have
extended science days there, and Callington staff come out to St
Mellion to do taster sessions.

Palin was delighted to discover that once her pupils get
to Callington they keep in touch with each other, forming a

St Mellion group inside the college, and last year the St Mellion Year 6 teacher went to Callington to meet her pupils now in Year 7 at Callington. 'It's a good school for all abilities,' says Palin. 'We have had some very able children who did not sit the eleven-plus to get into grammar school but went straight to Callington, and will do very well there.'

And here she touches on a running sore. There is no eleven-plus in Cornwall. But the border is less than 10 miles away, and Plymouth, just across it, has a selective system, an eleven-plus exam and three grammar schools. If children go to the grammar school, then 'off they go', says Palin. There's no mechanism for St Mellion to ease the transition, or stay in touch.

Results are good, though in 2008 not quite as good as Palin had hoped, and there is some rethinking going on. There were forty-two children in the class at one point, she points out, and in such a small school, a year cohort can be very small and one child who does not do well could account for a decline in the percentage.

The day starts with 'wake and shake' – moving to music in the playground. Palin normally joins in, but the day I was there she wore high heels in honour of my arrival. I think she was expecting to give it a miss, and was crestfallen just for a moment when our photographer pressed her to join the jumping and twisting, but she did it with good grace, and made a pretty good fist of it in the circumstances. 'You've got high shoes on today,' said the little boy twisting beside her, and she nailed a smile to her face, said something kindly and encouraging, and continued to torment her feet.

The whole school can fit into one classroom for assembly, and you get a feel of just how small it is and how comfortable everyone is with each other. Palin reads a story called 'The Mousehole', only it's not pronounced *mouse-hole*, she says, but *mowzle*. Why should that be? Hands shoot up all over the room to explain that it's because it's Cornish, and Mousehole, or Mowzle, is a village at the far end of the county, near Penzance.

Palin long ago got over any feeling of being an outsider in Cornwall, but the taxi driver who took me the 6 miles from the nearest town of Saltash was a reminder that this cannot have been easy. His family have lived in Saltash for generations and run its only taxi firm, and he would not leave 'my beloved Cornwall' for anything. He did consent to drive me across the border into Plymouth to get my train home, but he didn't really approve of anything that went on there, especially the taxi firms in Plymouth. He explained sadly that his son's new job was taking him a long, long way away from home. The poor lad has had to go and work in Bristol.

Tomorrow, continues Palin, there's something special happening. Do the children know what it is? They all know: the Christmas fair. 'Your mums and dads will have coffee and mince pies, and if you let them, they can have a glass of mulled wine. But only if you let them.' Hands go up. One child reports that her mother is bringing some Body Shop goods, another that his dad is running the lucky dip. 'And what happens to the money we raise?' asks Palin. The first child gets the answer wrong: no, it doesn't go to charity, it goes towards a fancy bit of kit for the school computer called a visualiser. And they have all been to the theatre recently, haven't they? Yes, yes, they saw *Scrooge*, and who was the famous performer they saw there? But here Palin, just for a moment, misjudges her audience. The name Tommy Steele works no magic with this audience. They quite liked the old fellow who danced and sang on the stage, all the same.

And at the end, there's a prayer. It's a legal requirement, and anyway this is a Church of England school, so Palin intones the Lord's Prayer and the children bow their heads and intone along with her. The place gets inspected by the Church as well as Ofsted, and she was once asked by a C of E luminary whether it would be a different sort of school if it were not a faith school. She got the line totally wrong, and is quite unrepentant about it. No, she said, it would be the same school. It was the community – the teachers, children and parents – who made the school what it was, not the Church of England.

She herself is not particularly religious – she describes herself as believing in Christian values, but since most of the things

Christians claim as Christian values are really universal values, like honesty and kindness, that tells us little. She certainly never aimed to run a faith school, though she is not unhappy doing so, but if the Church of England wanted a proselytising head teacher, they picked the wrong woman.

Still, not only is it a church school, but it's right beside the village church, and the vicar is a regular and much-valued visitor who often leads prayers in assembly. And while I was there, they were using the church to rehearse their nativity play. Not that it was the sort of nativity play most of us would recognise. Second World War evacuees were not, when I was a child, thought to have been regular visitors to the stable in Bethlehem. But the school is working on the 1930s and the war, and no chance to learn more about it is overlooked.

The federation with St Dominic, starting in January 2010, is partly in response to a government desire to federate schools under one head, which – though disguised with all sorts of management rhetoric – is really mostly a cost-saving measure. But it is also partly a response to problems at St Dominic which Cornwall Council thinks Palin is the ideal person to sort out.

It follows a year when she has been executive head at Quethiock, so she knows the downsides of being executive head of two schools instead of head at one. One of these is that she is not as integral to St Mellion as she used to be. 'Running one small school, you can have your mark on everything.' Another is the occasional painful clash. When I visited, she was struggling with the problem that both St Mellion and Quethiock had their carol services at the same time. She could not be at both, and neither could be shifted. She thought she would have to be at Quethiock because it was her last week there.

But the arrangement has its advantages for St Mellion too. More responsibility (and a better pay grade) for her able deputy is one of them, and funding for an extra half a teacher because Palin will no longer be able to take on class teaching is another.

Quethiock is a small church school about 7 miles from St Mellion, and rather more rural. St Dominic is 3 miles from

St Mellion and has wonderful views of Dartmoor and the river Tamar. In theory it is slightly bigger than St Mellion, with three classes instead of two, but it has been through a difficult patch and is under-subscribed, so it only has forty-seven children. 'The two schools are naturally friends,' says Palin.

It will be a 'soft' federation. Each school will have its own governing body, but they will share a head. Palin describes it as 'more like collaboration than federation', but the long-term thinking is for a 'hard' federation, merging the governing bodies. In the short term at least, St Dominic stands to gain more. It has poor outside facilities, and its children will be able to go to St Mellion, where they have splendid outdoor play equipment. 'I've got Rob and his bus, so I could bring the younger children to St Mellion,' says Palin. She adds:

> The teachers of the two schools will be able to meet and plan together. Teachers will be able to make contact and support each other. We will be able to rationalise better. For example, both schools have PE co-ordinators. One person can do that, and the other will be free to do more on other subjects.

St Dominic also has a remarkably unlovely building with no kitchen, and the day I was there, one of the rooms was unusable and the children were divided into two groups to eat their lunch in the classrooms. Teachers were supervising lunch, which is something Palin will put a stop to. Most of its children live in the village of St Dominick – the school's local reputation does not encourage people to make a journey there. Palin hopes to change all that. Success breeds success, and since winning the Head Teacher of the Year award she is something of a local celebrity, a reputation which she thinks will help bring more applications to St Dominic, together with the association with the well-regarded St Mellion.

She's not starting from scratch. The school came out of special measures in 2006 and Ofsted rated it as satisfactory in 2008. 'It is a happy school and pupils feel very safe and well cared for,' said the report. But there is some way to go, says Palin, and the challenge has given her a new lease of life. 'I've been at St Mellion for seven years, I appointed most of the staff, and I was starting to wonder what came next.' Now she knows.

Des Smith
The head as scapegoat

Des Smith was a lionised head teacher. Everyone wanted to know
him. In 1984 he became the head of the boys' school Bishop Ward
School, which under his leadership became the co-educational All
Saints Technology College. It's in the London Borough of Barking
& Dagenham, and Smith said towards the end of his 21-year
tenure: 'Barking & Dagenham is a tough area in which to work.
For example, it has the lowest number of graduates per household
in the whole of England and Wales. Numbers staying on in
education post-16 have been historically low.'

All Saints is a Catholic school, but it enjoys few of the normal
benefits of faith schools, as Smith explained: 'The Brentwood
diocese includes several former grammar schools and high-
achieving comprehensives. All Saints has historically been the
Cinderella of the diocese, not the school of choice for many
Catholic parents.'

These quotes come from a long panegyric to Smith in a 2005
book called *Excellence in Education: The Making of Great
Schools*, by Sir Cyril Taylor and Conor Ryan. Taylor was then
chairman of the Specialist Schools and Academies Trust (SSAT)
and the businessman chosen to advise on specialist schools by
both Conservative and New Labour education secretaries, and
Ryan had been an adviser to Tony Blair's first education secretary,
David Blunkett, and was to become education adviser to Blair
himself. Taylor managed to be an education guru to both Blair
and Margaret Thatcher. So it is no surprise that their book proved,
entirely to their own satisfaction, that the best people to control
schools are people who have demonstrated their worth by making

loads of money; that the old Labour notion of comprehensive education was far too uniform a solution; and that all children ought to be forced to wear school uniforms.

Within a year of the book's publication, Taylor was furiously distancing himself from the head he had praised so lavishly. Smith's downfall would prove to be his association with the SSAT, which just goes to show that the talents that go to make a good head teacher and those which enable a person to survive in politics are not the same, though they sometimes overlap.

Taylor and Ryan's praise for Smith was entirely justified by his record. In 1984, Bishop Ward School's results were very poor. It was under-subscribed with only around seventy-five pupils in each year group – about 460 overall in a school that should have had 800 – because no one would send their children there unless they had to. The place was very violent – no one felt safe there.

Smith stopped the rot, but did not achieve transformation overnight because that was not achievable. In 1994, just under a third of the pupils – 31 per cent – achieved five or more good grades at GCSE, which is hardly impressive but better than it had been when Smith took over, ten years earlier. By 1999 the figure had risen to 42 per cent, and then there was a spurt: by 2004 it was 85 per cent. In 2003 it was the most improved school in the country, and in 2005 about fifty of its pupils went to university. Ofsted visited that year and observed: 'Pupils' attitudes, behaviour and relationships are consistently very good; pupils want to learn.' Pupils told Ofsted inspectors they found the place safe, strict on behaviour, anti-bullying and friendly. The school was now over-subscribed; it had become the Catholic school of choice for the area.

How was it done? Taylor and Ryan only offer half the story. They quote Smith as saying: 'My first task was to end the violent atmosphere in the school and instil an ethos of non-violence, care and pastoral support.' But I asked Smith what he meant by violence, and it quickly became clear that before his arrival, this was a truly dangerous place to be. The corridors and playgrounds were controlled by gangs whom you did not cross, who extorted money with threats from other pupils. 'There was a kind of agreement between staff and boys – you leave us alone, we'll leave you alone. One boy forced a cricket bat handle up another's anus. It was dreadful stuff, an ugly atmosphere.' The last head had left three years previously, and there had only been an acting head all that time. Things were far, far worse than you would realise from Taylor and Ryan's account.

These were still the days when corporal punishment was legal, and it was especially prevalent in Roman Catholic schools. Bishop Ward School was known as the biggest beater in the borough. Of course only the stronger teachers could get boys to bend down and be beaten – the boys would tell other teachers to go away, though not in exactly those words – so the other teachers did not use their canes and had no authority at all, since the only authority there was came from beating.

One of Smith's first actions was to abolish corporal punishment. For this he faced a vote of no confidence among his staff, but the National Union of Teachers persuaded their members to give the new head a chance. 'Once violence from teachers stopped, I felt the whole atmosphere changed,' Smith said. It's interesting that there were still teachers in the 1980s who said they could not keep order without the cane, yet all the anecdotal evidence suggests that the very presence of beating in a school makes discipline very hard to maintain.

Next Smith expelled four of the ringleaders. This was not easy; parents wrote furiously to the governors, and hired lawyers and took the school to court. Smith had the full support of his governors, and says none of what he achieved would have been possible without it. 'I had brilliant governors, and you have to have that. When the going gets tough and parents write to complain, saying "My son's done nothing and he's excluded him", you need your governors.' The expulsions got rid of the hard core, and 'my constant mantra after that, in assemblies and everywhere I went, was: we are a non-violent school. Bullying meant exclusion for ten days. That was a pain for parents, who used to ring up and complain.'

There was no point in trying to do everything at once. In his first five years, from 1984 until 1989, Smith concentrated on setting down clear guidelines about behaviour, and cheerfully admits he did not trouble too much about the curriculum. That would come later, when he had created a place where learning could happen. He insisted on respect for teachers, and made pupils call them 'Sir' and 'Madam' and stand up when they walked into the room. It all gave the staff confidence, he says.

Those were also the years when he needed to win the hearts and minds of pupils and their parents. That meant holding regular parents' evenings, preparing them carefully to make sure they were attractive and interesting, and working hard to make sure parents came. By 2004 he was routinely getting nine out of ten parents. It meant making himself regularly available to parents, and he offered to do practical non-school things for them, like signing passport and driving licence applications. It meant being highly visible around the corridors, and holding assemblies which sounded a bit like revivalist meetings. It meant getting talented teachers, which every successful head says is the real key. Smith involved the school in Initial Teacher Training and had thirty trainee teachers a year; helping to train new teachers was good for his existing staff, he says, and from those thirty trainees he recruited some of his best new teachers. It also meant actively campaigning and fundraising for new buildings for science, music and drama.

Winning hearts and minds also meant a new induction programme for pupils in Year 7 – the first year in secondary school – in their first seven weeks in the school, including awaydays. 'If you capture the hearts and minds of these pupils in their first seven weeks you have them for their school career,' says Smith. On their first day in the school new pupils brought in their primary school workbooks, so that the teachers could see what they had been doing and to what standard. There was a special programme for those who arrived at the school still finding it hard to read or write.

As the school's standing improved, he started speaking about it from the pulpit at Mass every Sunday, for this was a Roman Catholic school and Mass was the place where he would meet his prospective parents. The priest was very supportive, allowing him to get up in the pulpit and talk about the improvements in his school, and to ask parents to come and give it another chance. 'I started to get aspiring parents who wanted to do well by their children,' he says. Gradually the reputation of the school grew better, the roll increased to 700, and he entered the 1990s with confidence that they were going to be a lot better than the 1980s. But he had not done everything in five years, by any means. 'This idea Cyril Taylor has of a hero head going in and doing it all in five years is nonsense,' Smith says.

The big breakthrough came in 1992, when he merged the school with a nearby Catholic girls' school, to make a co-educational school renamed All Saints. When Smith and the nun who headed the girls' school proposed the merger, the staff in both places were against it. It must have been a harder sell at the girls' school, for a boys' school always has more to gain from such a merger. As one wise and experienced teacher once put it to me, 'Everyone wants a mixed school for their sons and a single-sex school for their daughters.' But both schools were in a precarious position, and neither was yet off the danger list. It was a chance, perhaps a last chance, for both of them.

At first, and for four years, they worked on two sites, 4 miles apart, with teachers shuttling by minibus between the sites. But already the difference was being felt. Boys and girls were sitting beside each other, learning and showing mutual respect. Eventually there was a new building on the old boys' school site. The merger, for Smith, was the main event, if there was one, which made his school the calm, safe community it eventually became. However, the Taylor and Ryan account makes the crucial event something that happened two years later: the announcement that the school was to be one of the first forty technology colleges in Britain.

The school was certainly helped by the extra money which the government made available to schools which agreed to become technology colleges, a course of action which Taylor was urging upon schools. Smith remembers the occasion clearly. It was, in retrospect, the start of his cataclysmic fall.

I was sitting in a bar with Cyril Taylor as the then education secretary, Kenneth Baker, announced the names of the first forty schools to be given technology college status, and when we were chosen to be one of them, I was delighted and amazed. They threw money at you. After that I made a big push for technology, employing some brilliant IT teachers.

This, unsurprisingly, seemed to Taylor and Ryan to be the key factor and the key moment in the school's improvement. It meant 'prestigious sponsors' such as HSBC, though HSBC did not actually put money into the school. It meant, according to Taylor and Ryan, that All Saints 'felt it was part of a new breed of schools', but the meaning of this statement is not clear to me. Taylor and Ryan wrote that Smith paid tribute to the work of the SSAT. But Smith says: 'They would say that, because they think schools are businesses, but they are not.'

HSBC 'certainly did help us with financial planning, and gave us some very good support'. But the key factors, in Smith's view, were: ending the violence; the merger, which made the school co-educational; recruiting, training and keeping good teachers; and the fact that it was a faith school, which enabled him to turn it into what he calls 'a nice Christian community'. He says: 'Many of the pupils have wretched backgrounds but they can come to the school and feel safe and secure.' Despite Taylor's special pleading, there is no evidence that specialist status itself made much of a difference, but the extra money that came with it certainly did.

Taylor's admiration for Smith did not stop at words. He invited him to become an adviser to the SSAT, and to help in the task of finding commercial sponsors for schools. The SSAT's role had become terribly politically important for Tony Blair, who had set a target of 200 academies being open or under way by 2010. It was chaired by Blair's chief fundraiser and close friend Lord Levy, and its task was to seek out new donors and help them to set up academies.

And that was the cause of Smith's downfall.

In 2005, Smith was coming up for retirement – he was to retire the next year, at sixty – with a long and successful teaching career behind him. He was to leave loaded with the plaudits accorded to a head who has turned a sink school into a successful one. Instead, he went overnight from being a national treasure, whose success New Labour ministers liked to bask in, the valued friend not only of Sir Cyril Taylor but also of Lord Levy, to a national embarrassment whom they all tried to pretend they did not know. Here's how it happened.

In November 2005 a *Sunday Times* reporter approached the SSAT pretending that she represented a businessman interested in sponsoring an academy. The businessman was, in fact, a second undercover reporter using the name Malcolm Johnson. Taylor took the reporter to lunch in a private room at Mosimann's, an exclusive Knightsbridge restaurant in a converted church, and placed her next to Smith. The guests included Sir Michael Barber, former head of delivery at No. 10, two multi-millionaire businessmen and two representatives of an American multinational, as well as the academy sponsorship consultant Rona Kiley, wife of Bob Kiley, former head of Transport for London.

Smith expounded the benefits of the academy programme and suggested continuing the discussion over champagne at a bar in the heart of the City of London. The next day he emailed the undercover reporter, known as Claire, to thank her for a 'stimulating and enjoyable' evening. 'I would be very happy to facilitate a meeting with Malcolm to discuss the issues of sponsoring an academy.'

A few weeks later, at another top London restaurant, Johnson and Claire met Taylor, who said that Smith would be the perfect choice for Johnson to develop his academy project. But what was the payback, Johnson wanted to know. 'There's no question that sponsors of academies have access, they get invited to No. 10, meet the secretary of state and people like that,' said Taylor, who is the rare recipient of two knighthoods – one from the Tories and the other from Labour. He went on: 'Some people say "I'm going to buy a knighthood by doing this", but I think they should not think that at all because, first of all, that's a form of corruption. But the fact is a lot of sponsors do get recognition.'

Smith contacted Claire again in the new year. This time he suggested dinner and champagne back at the City wine bar. There, in April 2006, he seemed to set out a sort of tariff system, in which a benefactor who gave to 'one or two' academies might receive an OBE or a knighthood while a donor who funded five of them would be 'a certainty' for a peerage. 'The Prime Minister's office would recommend someone like Malcolm for an OBE, a CBE or a knighthood,' said Smith.

'Really? Just for getting involved with the academies?' asked the reporter.

'Just for, yes, they call them "services to education",' replied Smith. 'It's a nomination and then the Prime Minister would write to somebody and say "We're thinking of nominating you, but we'll choose the honour. It will either be an OBE, a CBE or a knighthood." I would say to Cyril's office that we've got to start writing to the Prime Minister's office.' For a donation of £10 million, 'you could go to the House of Lords'.

Two days later the *Sunday Times* reported Smith's comments under the headline 'Revealed: cash for honours scandal'.

Downing Street and Cabinet ministers moved quickly to distance themselves from Smith. Taylor rushed to tell the world that Smith was terribly low level, he didn't know anything, and the silly fellow got carried away. He did not know if Smith had ever met Levy, though he thought he probably had. He did not mention that Smith was one of his carefully chosen guests at a lunch to meet the *Sunday Times* reporter; Taylor, too, thought she was the PRO to a multi-millionaire.

The SSAT's official statement said:

Mr Smith's involvement with the SSAT was limited solely to educational matters. He was engaged as a consultant by SSAT to provide school improvement advice in relation to academies on two specific projects (which necessitated two days' work),

and he also acted as a consultant to the Department for
Education and Skills, to provide educational input on two
other projects in Bristol and in London.

The Metropolitan Police, the statement confirmed, had asked
the SSAT to assist them in their enquiries.

Even the defence secretary joined in the rush to tell the world
what an inconsequential fellow Smith was. John Reid said on
television: 'I don't know who Mr Des Smith is . . . He doesn't
speak with any authority for the government at all. As far as
I'm aware, he doesn't speak for the Labour Party either.' As Reid
spoke, the insignificant Mr Smith was being arrested at his home
and bailed. Downing Street said at the time that it was 'nonsense
to suggest that honours are awarded for giving money to an
academy'. Only his local MP, Jon Cruddas, had a good word
for him. Smith did a 'fantastic' job at his east London school,
said Cruddas.

Smith was arrested under the 1925 Honours (Prevention
of Abuses) Act as part of a wider police probe into alleged
corruption, which saw many of those closest to the Prime Minister
being arrested. The police turned up mob-handed at his home at
seven o'clock one morning and held him for six hours in the cells
while questioning him. It was a terrifying experience, he says.
He had been 'shattered by the experience. I was naive; I shouldn't
have said what I did. I'm desperately sorry.'

It was a miserable end to a distinguished teaching career.
He retired quietly, under a cloud, with none of the ceremonies
he might have expected. On 3 December 2006 Smith gave an
emotional interview to the *Mail on Sunday*, providing the front-
page story, in which he said: 'I demand that Blair is arrested
at 10 Downing Street at 7.20 a.m., that he is taken to a police
station – hopefully Stoke Newington, which is a very unpleasant
Bastille-type place – and treated the same way that I have been
treated.' His one comfort was that he never actually faced a court.
In February 2007 the Crown Prosecution Service announced there
would be no charges, as it had 'insufficient evidence'.

Smith's life fell apart. He moved home to a secret destination, his marriage disintegrated, and on 25 July 2006 he pleaded guilty to a drink-driving offence arising from an incident when he was found to be almost three times over the limit after his car crashed and ended up on its side. Smith was banned from driving for three years, fined £1,800 and ordered to attend a drink-impaired drivers' course and carry out eighty hours' community service.

It has taken him years to recover. But today, I am pleased to be the first writer he has been willing to speak to, and to report that he has regained some of his old bounce, and can talk about how he turned round a failing school with all of his old pride.

Kelly Gauld
The youngest head

Is Kelly Gauld, appointed head of Hillside Primary School in
Lower Earley, near Reading, in February 2009, aged just twenty-
nine, the youngest head teacher in Britain? We can't be sure, but
she does not know of a younger one. In fact, she was already
running the school at twenty-eight – she became acting head
in September 2008. She was certainly the youngest head at the
November 2009 New Heads Conference, and the 2009 report
on the state of the labour market for senior school staff prepared
for the National Association of Head Teachers (NAHT) and the
Association of School and College Leaders (ASCL) by Professor
John Howson makes it clear that the average head is quite a lot
older, especially if she is female:

> Five hundred and eleven schools provided us with
> details of the age of their new head teacher. This year,
> only 9 per cent, or forty-eight appointments, went to those
> aged under thirty-five, compared with 11 per cent last year
> and 13 per cent two years ago. However, the percentage
> aged between thirty-five and thirty-nine rose slightly to
> 29 per cent this year. Thus, the total appointed before
> their fortieth birthday amounted to 38 per cent this year,
> some four percentage points higher than last year. Those
> in their forties accounted for 44 per cent of appointments
> with 18 per cent, almost one in five, appointed after their
> fiftieth birthday.
>   Younger teachers were less likely to be appointed in
> foundation Roman Catholic schools and more likely to have

been appointed to community schools and voluntary Church of England schools.

Gauld is, however, a part of an increasing trend for young women teachers to have higher aspirations than they used to. More than a third (36 per cent) are now looking to become head teachers, a 16 per cent increase on last year, according to the National College for Leadership of Schools and Children's Services. As more women come forward to take on headships, there is a decline in the number of unfilled head teacher vacancies.

Just four months after her appointment, in June 2009, Gauld gave birth to her first child, a daughter. A message appeared on the school website: 'A very big welcome to little Polly Suzzanah Gauld, who made her arrival into the world yesterday, 1 June 2009, weighing in at 7lb 11oz.' Five weeks later, on 21 July, Gauld was back at work.

Was that hard for her? No, actually. 'I was ready to go back,' she told me on the telephone one evening in December, holding the receiver in one arm and Polly in the other, and trying to prevent her daughter from taking over the conversation. 'I was at home, sterilising bottles, and I thought, "I'm sure I was in charge of something before this."' She's not, she says, one of those people who are fulfilled by having children. She always knew she would want to go back to work quickly after Polly was born.

Gauld took a three-year teaching degree at Kingston University, starting with English and drama and changing to history and geography. Why change? Because she felt English and drama was too easy for her. 'I like to challenge myself.' Britain's youngest head – as we will call her until a challenger appears – does not suffer from false modesty.

In her first primary school, in Slough, she quickly became head of Year 5 and Year 6, and maths co-ordinator. From there she was appointed to develop maths teaching using interactive whiteboards in eighteen local schools. She was deputy head at Hillside for two years before becoming acting head in September 2008, whereupon she found herself in charge of a bigger than average school, with 456 pupils and a large nursery. It didn't have a particularly difficult intake – the proportion of pupils with learning difficulties is below average at one in ten, and just 10 per cent are poor enough to qualify for free school meals. Just under a third are from minority ethnic backgrounds, and for seventy-nine of her children, English is still a new and strange language. It's a very mixed intake, including some deprived areas. There is no selection at all; first priority goes to children who live within the catchment area, and then to those with brothers or sisters at the school.

Hillside had been in trouble and had been identified by Ofsted as needing significant improvement, but Gauld's predecessor had put things right. So when she started, it already had a clean bill of health and was over-subscribed, with a waiting list. All the same, Gauld arrived with characteristic restless energy and a list of things she wanted to change. Top of her list was to improve outdoor learning. 'We have an amphitheatre and a pond area and I was saying: "Why are we not using these places?" I have a working party of parents and governors who are clearing it all. The plan is for children to use it for play and for enriching the curriculum.' The curriculum is topic based, and the outdoor area will reflect the topics – Africa in Year 4, the Aztecs in Year 5. She is also keen to offer what she calls a life skills programme – the domestic and other skills we all need to get by.

That restless energy seems to be her defining characteristic. Some of the parents say she's a dynamo and ask where she gets her energy from. She says a head teacher ought to be like that: 'You get knocked over and you get up again.'

Gauld sings a lot, especially in assemblies. 'I love singing. I'm working with the music co-ordinator to get a musical culture in the school.' When she's not in school or looking after Polly, she's riding horses – she owns two, which, like her school and her daughter, require a lot of work and attention. She rides competitively, and was competing in dressage events eleven days after her daughter was born.

Kelly Gauld is half Irish and half Polish, so her single mother, living on a council estate in Hillingdon, west London, naturally brought her up in the Roman Catholic Church. 'Education was very important to my mum. My brother and I went to school and learned to read and write. Ours were the only divorced parents in our school.' She is still a churchgoer, but these days it's the Church of England – a compromise between her Catholicism and her husband's Scottish Presbyterianism.

She wants her staff to be as concerned about education as her mother was. 'One of the most important things for a teacher is to be passionate about education. But you must also have a passion outside school. Then you will be able to put that passion into your teaching. You need to be able to enjoy it.' She also wants risk takers. 'You must be willing to try something in the classroom and see what happens.' So in 2010 she is issuing five risk cards to all her teachers, and they must use them all. The cards will specify the risk to be taken – for example, to let the children plan a lesson, or to avoid using the interactive whiteboard for a whole week, or to spend a whole day outside. 'We are a can-do school. We always say, we can do it, whatever it is.' Gauld bubbles with enthusiasm about it. For me, as an outsider, it's infectious and exciting. I am not sure, though, if I were one of her staff, that I might not find it just the tiniest bit tiresome.

The same enthusiasm is going to go into the school rebuilding. Hillside Primary School was built in 1986, opening its doors for the first time in September that year, and half of it is due to be rebuilt. I don't envy the builders.

Index